ASK THE RABBI

WOMEN RABBIS RESPOND

TO

MODERN HALAKHIC QUESTIONS

by

D1506989

Monique Susskind Goldberg

and

Diana Villa

edited by

David Golinkin and Israel Warman

The Center for Women in Jewish Law

and

The Rabbi Israel Levinthal Center
for the Study of Contemporary Responsa
at the

Schechter Institute of Jewish Studies

Jerusalem 2010

ISBN
978-965-7105-66-5

Distribution:
The Schechter Institute of Jewish Studies
POB 16080, Jerusalem 91160 Israel

Tel.: 074-7800-600
Fax: 02-6790840
Email: schechter@schechter.ac.il
Website: www.schechter.edu

Produced by Leshon Limudim Ltd., Jerusalem
Tel. 02-537-2212 E-mail: leshon@netvision.net.il

Printed in Israel

This book has appeared

thanks to a generous grant

from the David Berg Foundation

About the Authors and Editors

Rabbi Monique Susskind Goldberg has been a Research Fellow at the Center for Women in Jewish Law at the Schechter Institute since 1999. Her publications include *The Jewish Law Watch, To Learn and To Teach, Za'akat Dalot: Halakhic Solutions for the Agunot of Our Time* and *Ask the Rabbi*.

Rabbi Diana Villa has been a Research Fellow at the Center for Women in Jewish Law at the Schechter Institute since 1999. Her publications include *The Jewish Law Watch, To Learn and To Teach, Za'akat Dalot: Halakhic Solutions for the Agunot of Our Time* and *Ask the Rabbi*. In addition, she is a Lecturer in Jewish Law at the Schechter Rabbinical Seminary and Schechter's representative on ICAR, the International Coalition for Agunah Rights.

Rabbi Prof. David Golinkin is the President and Jerome and Miriam Katzin Professor of Jewish Studies at the Schechter Institute of Jewish Studies where he also directs the Center for Women in Jewish Law. He is the author or editor of over forty books and numerous articles including *The Responsa of the Va'ad Halakhah, Responsa in a Moment,* and *The Status of Women in Jewish Law: Responsa*.

Rabbi Israel Warman is a Lecturer in Talmud and Jewish Law at the Schechter Rabbinical Seminary. He also serves as Faculty Advisor to the Center for Women in Jewish Law.

TABLE OF CONTENTS

INTRODUCTION

A recent bibliography of the *responsa* literature published by the Schechter Institute of Jewish Studies (Shmuel Glick, *Kuntress Hateshuvot*, Jerusalem, 2006-2009) lists approximately 4,500 collections of *responsa* published between the years 1470 and 2000.

Even so, this volume of *responsa* is "different from all other *responsa*" in a number of ways.

First of all, it is the first volume of *responsa* in history written by two women rabbis. This is a natural result of the growing participation of women in Jewish learning during the past ninety years and of the ordination of women as Conservative rabbis since 1985.

Second, like many of the *responsa* written by Conservative rabbis since 1913 (see my book *The Responsa of Professor Louis Ginzberg*, New York and Jerusalem, 1996, p. 24), these *responsa* are written in English.

Third, the *responsa* in this volume are expanded versions of over ninety *responsa* out of approximately 600 *responsa* written on the *Ask the Rabbi* website of the Schechter Institute of Jewish Studies. This is part of the proliferation of "Ask the Rabbi" websites which may over time have a transformative effect on the *responsa* literature as a whole.

Finally, many of the questions on that website and in this book were asked by non-Jews who wanted to know what Judaism has to say about various topics. This too has precedents in modern times (see *The Responsa of Professor Louis Ginzberg*, pp. 24-25), but the phenomenon has clearly grown as a result of the Internet.

These *responsa* originally appeared in a very concise form on the *Ask the Rabbi* website between 2002-2010. For this volume, Rabbis Monique Susskind Goldberg and Diana Villa selected some of the most interesting *responsa*, expanded them, and added sources and bibliography together with the help of Rabbi Israel Warman. I then edited the *responsa* and added additional bibliography. It should be stressed that each *responsum* repre-

11

sents the opinion of the author and not necessarily of the four rabbis involved in writing this volume.

Since these *responsa* were written for Jewish laypeople and non-Jews, they are not organized in the traditional fashion according to the order of the *Shulḥan Arukh*, but rather in alphabetical order by category such as Bible, Conversion, Ethics and Morality and so on.

We have added a Glossary of terms, authors and titles in order to assist readers unfamiliar with Jewish Law.

In conclusion, we would like to thank the donors who have supported the Center for Women in Jewish Law over the years, especially the Ford Foundation and the Dorot Foundation, as well as the David Berg Foundation, which gave a generous gift to support the publication of this volume. This volume was also funded by the Rabbi Israel Levinthal Center for Contemporary Responsa at the Schechter Institute.

We hope that this volume will serve to encourage more Jews to "Ask the Rabbi" and more women to get involved in studying and writing about *halakhah*.

David Golinkin
Schechter Institute of Jewish Studies
Jerusalem
Elul 5770 – September 2010

BIBLICAL STUDIES

1. How Did the *Urim* and *Tumim* Work?

QUESTION

Dear Rabbi,

How did the *Urim* and *Tumim* work?

ANSWER

Very little is known about the nature or the form of the *Urim* and *Tumim*. The only thing mentioned in the Bible is that they were divinatory objects put in the Breastplate of Judgment (*Ḥoshen Hamishpat*) worn by the High Priest (see Exodus 28:30). Scholars believe that there were two stones or pieces of parchment, with the inscriptions *Urim* on one and *Tumim* on the other (see For Further Reading below).

The exact meaning of the words is also not known. Some scholars believe *Urim* comes from the same root as *arr* [curse] and *Tumim* from *tmm* [faultless]. If so, the *Urim* and *Tumim* are used essentially as a way to cast lots and to decide, for example, if a person is guilty or innocent.

Scholars tend to agree that the two words have opposite meanings, thus allowing a positive or negative answer (see *Encyclopaedia Judaica; Olam Hatanakh*). In the examples described in the Bible, it seems that the question has to be simple, requiring a yes or no answer (see for instance Numbers 27:21; I Samuel 14:36-37; *Yoma* 73a).

In rabbinic sources, there is an opinion that *Urim* comes from the Hebrew root *or* [light] and *Tumim* from the Hebrew root *tum* [complete]. This would lead to a translation of "light and perfection" and their function would be the revelation of truth (*Sifrei Zutra* 27:21; *Yoma* 73b).

The Babylonian Talmud (*Yoma* 73a-b) and the *Rishonim* commenting on this passage have a more elaborate explanation of the way the High Priest used the *Urim* and *Tumim* (see Rashi to *Yoma ad loc., s.v. boltot*; Maimonides, Laws of the Temple Utensils and Their Users 10:11 and Ritva, *Yoma* 73b, *s.v. ha de'amrinan*.

According to this explanation, *Urim* and *Tumim* refer to special names of God and are placed in the fold of the breastplate worn by the High Priest. On the breastplate were 12 stones inscribed with the names of the 12 tribes. According to the Babylonian Talmud (*ibid.*), to complete the alphabet, the names of the patriarchs, Avraham, Yitzhak and Ya'akov, as well as the words *Shivtei Yeshurun* [Tribes of Yeshurun] were also inscribed on the stones.

When a question was brought before the High Priest, he would meditate on the Holy Name of the *Urim*. This would cause some of the letters on the stones of the breastplate to protrude. These letters formed the answer to the question. However, since the letters were not in any special order, the High Priest would then meditate on the Holy Name of the *Tumim* and in doing so, would receive Divine inspiration as to how to arrange the letters properly and thus answer the question.

Although the answer of the Talmud and the *Rishonim* is fascinating and beautiful, I personally tend to accept the modern scholars' opinion that the *Urim* and *Tumim* were a method of casting lots.

Rabbi Monique Susskind Goldberg
April 2007

FOR FURTHER READING

1. *Encyclopaedia Judaica*, second edition, Jerusalem, 2007 ,"*Urim* and *Thummim*", vol. 20, pp. 422-423.

2. *Entziklopedia Mikra'it*, "*Urim Vetumim*", vol. 1, Jerusalem, 1950, pp. 179-183 [Hebrew].

3. *Olam Hatanakh, Shemot*, Tel Aviv 1992, pp. 172-173 [Hebrew].

2. Is Cannabis Mentioned in the Bible?

QUESTION

Dear Rabbi,

My seventeen-year-old, who is an advocate of cannabis, read an article entitled "Jesus Used Marijuana". The article claims that the oil with which Jesus was anointed was made from the same ingredients that are described in Exodus 30:23. The article posits that two of these plants, *qinman bosem* and *qneh bosem*, often translated as sweet cinnamon and fragrant cane, are in fact cannabis. Is this true?

Distraught Mom

ANSWER

There is indeed a strong similarity in the **sound** of the words *kinman bosem, qneh bosem* and cannabis. However, they are not connected linguistically.

According to Professor Yehudah Feliks, a well-known expert on Biblical and talmudic botany, *qinman bosem* is cinnamon, while *qneh bosem* is a tropical plant, most probably *andropogon nardus*, a fragrant reed from India.

Cannabis is a genus of a plant from the *canabacea* family. It is known in English as hemp and is unrelated to the plants mentioned in Exodus 30.

The word cannabis is from the Greek *kannabis* (κάνναβις). The Hebrew words *"qinman bosem"* and *"qneh bosem"* are not connected to it.

I hope that this information is useful in convincing your son that he is mistaken.

Sincerely,
Rabbi Diana Villa
October 2004

FOR FURTHER READING

1. Feliks, Yehudah, *Nature and Land in the Bible*, Jerusalem, 1992, pp. 59-60 [Hebrew].

2. *idem*, *Plant World of the Bible*, Tel Aviv, 1957, p. 268 [Hebrew].

3. Partridge or Cuckoo?

QUESTION

Dear Rabbi,

Rashi's commentary on I Samuel 26:20 explains that the *Kore* is a bird called *Perdix* in Latin (Partridge in English). Rashi states that this bird acts peculiarly by looking for other birds' nests in order to sit on their eggs. Similarly, he says that the *Kore* mentioned in Jeremiah 17:11 is also the Perdix. However, in his commentary on the verse in Jeremiah, Rashi states that the *Kore* is the bird called *Coucou* in French, or Cuckoo in English. Why the confusion regarding the two distinct types of birds?

I find a second contradiction in Rashi's commentary on *Ḥullin* 140b, which implies that the *Kore* is a pure (kosher) bird, while it is known that the Cuckoo is an impure bird (non-kosher). And finally, what is most difficult for me is that Rashi's identifying the *Kore* with the Cuckoo goes against Nature's Laws. The Cuckoo does **not** sit on other birds' eggs. In fact, it has the habit of putting its own eggs in other birds' nests. Can you please help me understand these contradictions in Rashi?

ANSWER

It is always fascinating to try and identify the animals which appear in the Bible. According to the experts cited in the *Entziklopedia Mikra'it*, and according to Prof. Yehudah Feliks, the *Kore* is a bird from the Partridge family (more specifically: *Ammoperdix Heyi*), which has the habit of laying its eggs in nests on the ground. Often a few females lay their eggs in the same nest, and one of them sits on the eggs. This could explain the meaning of the verse in Jeremiah (17:11): "Like a partridge hatching what she did not lay". In other words, the *Kore* raises chicks to which she did not give birth.

According to rabbinic sources, the *Kore* is considered an "*of tahor*" (pure/kosher bird) (see *Mishnah Ḥullin* 12:2 and *Tosafot* on *Ḥullin* 63a, *s.v. netz*).

Let's now examine Rashi. In every place where the *Kore* is mentioned in the Bible and in the Talmud, Rashi identifies it

19

rightfully with the *Perdix* (in old French), or the Partridge. The only exception is in his commentary on Jeremiah, where he identifies the Kore with the Cuckoo. According to Yitzḥak Avinery, an expert on Rashi, Rashi changed his mind in his commentary to Jeremiah 17:11.

We can see this in his commentary on *Ḥullin* 140a (*s.v. R. Eliezer*), where Rashi states that the *Kore* is a pure bird and is **not** the one called Cuckoo [*"of tahor hu velo zehu shekorin kuku"*]. This fits Rashi's commentary *ibid.* (*s.v. dilma*), where he explains that when the Talmud speaks about a pure bird sitting on pure eggs [*tahor vetahor*], it is referring to the *Kore*.

This last commentary of Rashi seems to contradict another of his commentaries on folio 140a (*s.v. Kore*) where in our versions in the printed Talmud he said that the kore is *tameh* (impure/not kosher). According to Avinery, in the original version of Rashi's commentary on *Ḥullin* 140a, he does not state that the *Kore* is *tameh* [impure], as we have in our version. He just states that the *Kore* is a bird whose habit is to sit on the eggs of others.

In conclusion, the *Kore* mentioned in the Bible and in the Talmud is of the Partridge family, even according to Rashi.

All the best,
Rabbi Monique Susskind Goldberg
April 2002

FOR FURTHER READING

1. Avinery, Yitzḥak, *Heikhal Rashi*, vol. 2, Jerusalem, 1985, p. 298 [Hebrew].

2. *Entziklopedia Mikra'it*, *"Kore"*, vol. 7, Jerusalem, 1976, pp. 215-216 [Hebrew].

3. Feliks, Yehudah, *Plants and Animals of the Mishnah*, Jerusalem, 1983, p. 276 [Hebrew].

4. What Happened to the *Nun* in *Ashrei*?

QUESTION

Dear Rabbi,

In the prayer *"Ashrei yoshvei veytekha,"* the sentences begin alphabetically, i.e. the first with *aleph* and the second with *bet* and so on, but when we get to *mem*, we skip *nun* and go to *samekh*. What happened to the *nun*?

ANSWER

Psalm 145 is an acrostic poem, each verse beginning with the successive letters of the Hebrew alphabet from *alef* to *tav*. But as you observed, the verse beginning with a *nun* is lacking. Scholars are divided on the question if this verse was missing from the start or was lost.

In the Septuagint Greek translation of the Bible (dated around the third century BCE), and in the Psalms Scroll found in Qumran (cave 11, dating 30-50 CE), there **is** a verse in this Psalm beginning with *nun*.

In the Septuagint we read: *"ne'eman Adonai bekhol devarav vehasid bekhol ma'asav [Adonai* is faithful in all his words and gracious in all his works]" (from the 1851 English version of the LXX by L.C.L. Brenton; see also *Biblia Hebraica*, Stuttgart, 1967/ 77, p. 1223, note on verse 13). The first word of the verse was thus *"ne'eman"* [faithful].

In the Qumran Psalms Scroll, we have a similar verse with some differences: *"ne'eman Elohim bidevarav vehasid bekhol ma'asav [Elohim* is faithful in His words and gracious in all His works]. This verse is very similar to the one found in the Septuagint and, aside from the first word, is very similar to verse 17 of our version: *"Tzadik Adonai bekhol derakhav vehasid bekhol ma'asav"* [*Adonai* is righteous in all His ways and gracious in all His works]. This similarity between the verse beginning with a *nun* (from Qumran and from the Septuagint) and verse 17 from our version has been interpreted in two ways by scholars. Either the verse was added to complete the acrostic poem, or it was originally there, but was taken out because of its similarity to verse 17.

Even if there was a version with a verse beginning with a *nun* in antiquity, by in the time of the Talmud, it had disappeared, and this abnormality begged for an explanation, as we see from *Berakhot* 4b.

Rabbi Yoḥanan noted the lack of a verse beginning with *nun* and explained that the letter *nun* is used in the verse in Amos (5:2) *"naflah lo tosif kum, betulat Yisrael"* ["The virgin of Israel is fallen, she shall rise no more"] speaking about the downfall of Israel. According to Rabbi Yoḥanan, King David, the author of Psalm 145, did not want to include in his psalm a verse starting with a *nun* because it would remind one of the downfall of Israel. Rav Naḥman bar Yitzḥak adds that although David did not want to write a verse about the downfall of Israel, he knew by prophetic vision that this would happen. Therefore, wanting to bring consolation to those who would fall, he wrote in verse 14, a verse of consolation: "The Lord upholds all that fall..." [*"somekh Adonai lekhol hanoflim"*].

In conclusion, it seems that we will never know for sure what happened to the *nun* in *Ashrei*!

Rabbi Monique Susskind Goldberg
January 2003

FOR FURTHER READING

1. Benovitz, Moshe, *Talmud Ha-igud, Berakhot*, Chapter 1, edited by Shamma Friedman, Jerusalem, 2006, pp. 158-159 [Hebrew].

2. "No *nun* in *Ashrei*", http://onthemainline.blogspot.com/2006/06/no-nun-in-ashrei.html

3. *Olam Hatanakh, Tehillim*, vol. 2, Tel Aviv, 1995, p. 268 [Hebrew].

4. Williams, Tyler F., "11Q5 (11QPsa) Qumran Psalms Scroll" http://biblical-studies.ca/dss/dss-introductions/81-1195.html

5. Who are the Cutheans?

QUESTION

Dear Rabbi,

What exactly is a Cuthean?

ANSWER

At the end of the 8th century BCE, when the Assyrian Kings Shalmaneser V and, after him, Sargon II and Sennacherib invaded the Kingdom of Israel, the Ten Tribes living there were exiled to Assyria and different people were brought in their stead to the cities of Samaria, among them the Cutheans (see For Further Reading). After they settled in the cities of Samaria, those people were called in our sources the Samaritans (see for example *Pirkei deRabbi Eliezer, chap. 37; Yalkut Shimoni* on II Kings, parag. 234).

The Cutheans were brought from Cutah, an ancient Sumerian-Akkadian city. This city was identified in archaeological excavations in the 19th century and is situated some 30 kilometers northeast of the city of Babylon, today Baghdad in Iraq (see *Entziklopedia Mikra'it*).

Like the other Assyrian people settled in Samaria, the Cutheans brought with them their idols and worshipped them (see Josephus). The Biblical sources relate that when the then-sparsely populated areas became infested with dangerous wild beasts, the Cutheans appealed to the king of Assyria for Israelite priests to instruct them on how to worship the "God of that country". The result was the creation of a syncretistic religion, in which different national groups living in Samaria worshipped the Hebrew God, but they also served their own gods in accordance with the customs of the nations from which they had been brought (see II Kings 17:25-41).

The early Talmudic Sages are divided on the question whether the Cutheans were true converts or only converted out of fear (see *Kiddishin* 75b). In later Talmudic times, they were considered a community of idolaters (see *Ḥullin* 5b-6a) and

Israelites were not allowed to marry Cutheans (see *Ketubot* 29a and Rashi *ad loc., s.v. Cutit*).

From the 13th century on, the Catholic Church forced the Jews to eliminate from their books terms that supposedly blasphemed against Christianity. In the 16th century, an index was established by the Church that listed books which had to have passages revised or deleted before publication. Objectionable words like *goy* or *nokhri*, two terms meaning non-Jew that could be understood as Christians, had to be changed (see *Encyclopaedia Judaica*). This is why, in the printed editions of the Talmud, those words were turned into the word *Cuti* that came to refer to any idolaters, without relation to the original Cutheans.

Rabbi Monique Susskind Goldberg
April 2009

FOR FURTHER READING

1. *Encyclopaedia Judaica*, second edition, Jerusalem, 2007, "Censorship", vol. 4, pp. 539-541; "Cuth, Cuthah", vol. 5, pp. 344-345; "Exile, Assyrian", vol. 6, pp. 607-608; "Talmud, burning of", vol. 19, pp. 481-483.

2. *Entziklopedia Mikra'it*, *"Cut, Cutah"*, vol. 4, Jerusalem, 1962, pp. 73-74, and *"Shomronim"*, vol. 8, Jerusalem, 1982, pp. 146-147 [Hebrew].

3. Josephus Flavius, "The Antiquities of the Jews", IX, 14, 1-3, in *Josephus' Complete Works*, translated by William Whiston, fourteenth printing, USA, 1977, pp. 211-212.

CONVERSION

6. May a Homosexual Convert to Judaism?

QUESTION

Dear Rabbi,

Is it possible for practicing homosexuals to convert with the Conservative/Masorti movement? Would the impossibility of fulfilling the *mitzvah* of being fruitful and multiplying (*pru u'revu*) disqualify the candidate?

ANSWER

The only homosexual act which is clearly a Biblical prohibition is anal sex (see Leviticus 18:22 and 20:13; Maimonides, Laws of Forbidden Sexual Relations 1:14).

According to the sources, the candidate to conversion commits to keep the Commandments (see below, No. 13). Therefore, if a prospective candidate would openly reject this Biblical prohibition, he would not be accepted for conversion.

Most Conservative *Batei Din* (Rabbinic Courts) would not ask direct questions regarding sexual preference. Not having children would not be an impediment for conversion since you are not rejecting the *mitzvah* of having children in principle. Besides, it is possible that in the future you may fulfill this *mitzvah*.

Sincerely,

Rabbi Diana Villa
July 2004

FOR FURTHER READING

Allen, Wayne, *Perspectives on Jewish Law and Contemporary Issues*, Jerusalem, 2009, No. 47, pp. 241-243.

7. May a Hunter Convert to Judaism?

QUESTION

Dear Rabbi,

As a Noahide seriously considering converting to Judaism, I have a
question that is really bothering me
and I don't know where to look to
find the answer. I hope you can help.

I am an avid deer hunter and firm
believer in a "clean kill." By that, I
mean a solid heart shot so the animal does not feel any pain. I
have passed on more deer than I have shot for this very reason.
Also, I do not believe in hunting for sport. I hunt for the meat and
enjoy eating it. I have read the Torah on this and have found
Leviticus 17:13:

> And if any Israelite or any stranger who resides among
> them hunts down an animal or a bird that may be eaten, he
> shall pour out its blood and cover it with earth.

Based on this, hunting is allowed. However, I have been told that
since hunting does not involve a *shohet* (a person who performs
ritual slaughter), it is not allowed. My understanding is that the
laws of the *shohet* apply to domesticated animals, not wild.

The bottom line here is: Is hunting allowed by Jewish law? If
not, why would the Torah suggest the proper/kosher way to
perform an improper/unkosher act?

Am I even on the right track here? If not, where would I need
to go to study more on this subject?

ANSWER

According to Jewish law, in order to eat meat, the animal must be
ritually slaughtered (*Yoreh De'ah* 13) and the meat is salted and
soaked in water (*ibid.* 69:1). Animals that are shot by a hunter and
not slaughtered are not kosher and therefore cannot be eaten.

The verse you quote should be understood to mean that, as in
the case of domesticated animals, if one hunts down a wild

28

animal, and then slaughters it, its blood cannot be consumed (see *Ḥullin* 28a; *Yoreh De'ah* 13:1).

Judaism does not, in general, approve of hunting. Rabbi Ezekiel Landau, for example, forbids recreational hunting. He considers this to be senseless destruction and cruelty to animals, besides having a negative effect on the hunter himself. He sees it as an activity of people of poor character such as Esau (Genesis 25:27 ff.) and Nimrod (*ibid.*, 9:8-9).

Some decisors allow hunting when it is for legitimate purposes that serve men, such as for leather, even without ritual slaughtering, but they definitely do not allow hunting for sport (see R. Israel Isserlein).

In conclusion, I believe that if you wish to continue hunting and eating the meat of the animal you shot, which contradicts a Biblical Law, you will not be able to convert to Judaism (see below, No. 13).

Sincerely,
Rabbi Diana Villa
May 2004

FOR FURTHER READING

1. *Encyclopaedia Judaica*, second edition, Jerusalem, 2007, "Hunting", vol. 9, pp. 621-622.

2. Isserlein, R. Israel, *Pesakim Uketavim*, No. 105 [Hebrew].

3. Landau, R. Ezekiel, *Responsa Noda Bi-Yehudah*, *Yoreh De'ah*, second series, No. 10 [Hebrew].

4. Novak, David, "The Sport of Hunting" in: *Law and Theology in Judaism*, New York, 1974, pp. 55-60.

5. Schochet, Elijah, *Animal Life in Jewish Tradition*, New York, 1984, pp. 158-159, 266-272.

8. May a Prospective Convert Wear a *Tallit* in the Synagogue?

QUESTION

Dear Rabbi,

Shalom, I am taking conversion classes in order to convert to Judaism, and I would like to know if I am allowed to wear a *tallit* in the synagogue. Once, an Orthodox rabbi told me that if I'm taking classes to convert I **should** wear one not only at home but in the synagogue as well, so I can put into practice the *mitzvot* I'm learning.

But I also know of some Orthodox congregations that don't let someone who is still in conversion classes wear it. What is your opinion?

ANSWER

A Jew is commanded to wear fringes on garments with four corners as a reminder of God's commandments (Numbers 15:37-41). In ancient times, when men wore as an outer garment a kind of rectangular mantle, Jews tied fringes to this mantel. When they moved to countries where people did not wear four-cornered cloaks, the Jews also changed the way they dressed and the fringes were tied to a prayer shawl, the *tallit*, which became a religious garment.

As long as you are not converted, you did not officially take the commandments upon yourself. Therefore, there is no obligation for you to wear a *tallit*. Nevertheless, there are rabbis who think that a prospective convert may wear the *tallit* as you have suggested, in order to practice the *mitzvah*.

On the other hand, other rabbis think that the use of the *tallit* should begin **after** the conversion ceremony. One of their arguments is that there may be some confusion in the synagogue, if the rabbi or *gabbai* thought that someone was Jewish because that person was wearing a *tallit* and asked that person to perform a ritual function during the service that that person may not yet be permitted to fulfill.

By wrapping yourself in a fringed garment for the first time after your conversion, you are symbolically showing that from that moment forward you accept the *mitzvot* (the fringes being a reminder of those *mitzvot*).

Although it is not forbidden for a non-Jew to wear a *tallit*, I personally tend to be of the opinion that it is more appropriate for a convert to wear the *tallit* in public **after** the completion of the conversion process. Therefore, wearing the *tallit* at home would be fine, but before you wear it in the synagogue, you should ask the rabbi of your synagogue about their policy on the subject.

I hope this is helpful.

Rabbi Monique Susskind Goldberg
October 2005

FOR FURTHER READING

1. CCAR *RESPONSA* 5765 (2005), 5 "May a Non-Jew Wear a *Tallit?"*, http://data.ccatnet.org/cgi-bin/respdisp.pl?file=5&year=5765

2. *Encyclopaedia Judaica*, second edition, Jerusalem, 2007, *"Tallit"*, vol. 19, pp. 465-466.

3. Freehof, Solomon B., *Reform Responsa for Our Time*, H.U.C. Press, 1977, No. 5, pp. 25-27.

4. Goldberg Susskind, Monique, *"Tallit* used by non-Jew", www.schechter.edu/askrabbi/symbol_tallit4.thm

5. Walter, Jacob, *Halakhah*, a publication of the Freehof Institute of Progressive *Halakhah*, Spring/Summer 1996.

9. May I Convert and Continue Acting?

QUESTION

Dear Rabbi,

Upon deciding (or "being decided" since *Hashem* undoubtedly had a part in it) to become a Jew through the Masorti/Conservative movement, I find myself faced with somewhat of a dilemma: I also wish to become an actress.

I have been encouraged by several drama teachers to pursue a career in acting, but always said "no" as I had, up until recently, imagined myself converting Modern Orthodox, and then not being able to combine the two.

Besides this, I am also a writer of poetry and prose (in Swedish, my first language) and I have been told that I have quite a promising future here as well. (I am by no means trying to show off, I just want to make it clear that I am not simply interested in these things for a hobby, nor am I, to be perfectly honest, unrealistic in my goals.)

While I love Judaism, I also love acting and writing.

My question is, therefore, could I, as an **observant** Conservative Jewess, act and write? What I really want to know is, besides working on the Sabbath and other holidays, where the answer is more obvious, is there any reason, philosophically so to speak, why I couldn't work in these fields, such as immodesty, or anything else I have not yet thought of? Would I have to select halakhicaly "OK" material, or could I pretty much be a "normal" actress, otherwise living a Jewish, Conservative, life?

Any help would be truly and greatly appreciated.

ANSWER

I can only answer your question with one big YES. Yes, you may pursue an artistic career in theatre and in writing and be an observant Jew; there is no contradiction. There are renowned observant writers and poets, such as S.Y. Agnon, Ḥayyim Sabbato, Zelda and Eliaz Cohen. There are observant actors such as Shuli Rand in the theatre and cinema and observant singers such as Dudu Fischer and Rabbi Shlomo Carlebach *z"l*. Judaism does not restrict the range of activities a person can do as long as one respects *halakhah*. There is no reason you could not write and act. As a religious person, you will feel yourself what are the borders you should not cross in the area of modesty, in your writings as well as in your acting. I believe that every actor selects the material that fits his/her personality. Being religious will naturally make you reject the material that does not fit your deep feelings.

The question of keeping Shabbat and the holidays may sometimes be an impediment in an acting career; you probably will have to reject certain roles. It's up to you to set your priorities.

Good luck in your conversion process, and continue to use your gifts, which also come from God, and by your creativity you enrich the world around you.

All the best,
Rabbi Monique Susskind Goldberg
June 2004

FOR FURTHER READING

1. Abrahams, Israel, *Jewish Life in the Middle Ages*, London, 1896, Chapters XIII-XIV.

2. *Encyclopaedia Judaica*, second edition, Jerusalem, 2007, "Theater", vol. 19, pp. 669-695.

3. Roth, Cecil, *The Jews in the Renaissance*, Philadelphia, 1959, Chapter XI, pp. 243-270.

10. May I Convert If My Husband Does Not Convert?

QUESTION

Dear Rabbi,

I desperately want an Orthodox conversion, but my husband is agnostic. He is happy to support me on my spiritual path, but does not want to convert himself. I cannot find a rabbi who will accept me! I would like to know what the policies of the Masorti Movement are concerning the conversion of someone already married to a Gentile. Will a Conservative Rabbi convert someone on the assumption that perhaps his/her partner may convert at some future time?

Thank you for your consideration.

ANSWER

There are several reasons why Rabbis are hesitant to accept a person into a conversion program when the spouse does not convert.

The conversion process, learning, examination by a *Beit Din* (rabbinical court), circumcision (for a man) and *mikveh*, is only the first step in becoming a Jew. Afterward, there is day-to-day life, observing the commandments of *kashrut*, keeping Shabbat and celebrating holidays. Even if your husband supports your spiritual path, can you ask him to change his life style? Can you request from him to keep the laws of *kashrut*? Will he abstain from driving on Shabbat to visit friends or family? If you become Jewish, your children born after your conversion will be Jewish. How will you educate them? How can you impose a traditional Jewish way of life on your family if your husband does not convert?

Another problem is that by converting while your husband does not, you are creating an interfaith marriage which is forbidden by Jewish Law (see *Even Ha'ezer* 16:1).

An answer was written in 1993 by a member of the Committee on Jewish Law and Standards of the Conservative Movement (in America), on the question of conversion of a person whose spouse does not intend to convert. The writer concludes that a person in that circumstance is accepted as a candidate to conversion because the mixed marriage is only a **consequence** of the conversion and not an active act of a Jew marrying a non-Jew.

This answer was not accepted by all the members of the Committee and even the rabbi who wrote this opinion states clearly that the convert "has a greater difficulty in fulfilling Jewish responsibility and achieving a Jewish lifestyle". He therefore continues:

> The Rabbi and the *Beit Din* who supervise and carry out the conversion have the responsibility to make sure that the non-converting spouse... is supportive of the convert and will cooperate with the convert in maintaining standards of *kashrut*, Shabbat and holiday observance... (see Bergman, p. 131).

Even if some rabbis are willing, in theory, to accept a person whose spouse does not convert, in practice, most rabbis will be hesitant to convert such a person.

It is our opinion that a rabbi should not agree to convert a person whose spouse does not convert, because the convert will not be able to live a full Jewish life, and will be transgressing during all his/her married life by having sexual relations with a non-Jew.

I hope I have helped a little in clarifying the issues.

All the best,

Rabbi Monique Susskind Goldberg
October 2004

FOR FURTHER READING

Bergman, Ben-Zion, "The Case of the Unconverted Spouse", *Responsa 1991-2000*, New York, 2002, pp. 127-131.

11. How May One Ensure Modesty at Outdoor Conversion Ceremonies?

QUESTION

Dear Rabbi,

My community does not have a *mikveh*, so conversion ceremonies are held at public beaches. Women are told to enter the water up to their neck, remove their bathing suits, immerse completely three times and recite the blessings in a prescribed manner. Male rabbis observe this; they do not bring female witnesses.

It is my understanding that rabbis officiating at conversions are required to hear the blessing; they are not required to *see* the actual dunking; the immersions must be witnessed by a properly trained and trusted person, a female in the case of female converts.

Recently there have been some problems with the conversion process in my community, resulting in less than dignified and modest experiences for female converts.

Please discuss the question of who should be the visual witness to immersion at conversions. If there is any source you can cite which addresses this, please include it. In addition, please advise on how to proceed to bring about change in the local rabbinate if you agree that change is needed.

ANSWER

The *Shulḥan Arukh* describes the immersion of a female convert as follows; my comments are in brackets:

> If she is is a woman, women seat her in the water up to her neck, and the *dayanim* are outside [the *mikveh* room], and they inform her of some of the minor and major *mitzvot* while she is seated in the water, and she then immerses in front of them [I suppose they come in when the woman is up to her neck in the water and they verify that she immersed completely]. They turn their faces and leave so they would not see her when she goes up (*Yoreh De'ah* 268:2).

36

It is clear from this that every consideration is made to ensure that the male *dayanim* would not see the nakedness of the woman. However, the *dayanim* should witness that the immersion is properly done. The act of immersion completes the conversion, not the blessing. In *mikvaot* nowadays, as you correctly point out, properly trained women witness that the dunking is completed while the *dayanim* remain in the adjoining room. They hear the *mikveh* woman say "kosher" after each of the three immersions and only then do they listen to the blessing.

For the situation you describe at a public beach, if you are not using women rabbis, then one could ask the *dayanim* to come close to the water only when the woman is ready to dunk (up to her neck in the water), and leave as soon as they hear the blessing. They should not be present while the woman takes her bathing suit off or comes out of the water. There is also a possibility for the woman to immerse while wearing a very loose garment (see *Yoreh De'ah* 198:46 and *Shakh*, subparag. 56).

I hope I have answered your question. I believe easy and dignified solutions can be found, such as providing big sheets or some other type of screen to insure the woman's personal privacy, especially when she enters and exits the water.

Rabbi Monique Susskind Goldberg
August 2006

FOR FURTHER READING

Ginzberg, Louis, *The Responsa of Professor Louis Ginzberg* edited by David Golinkin, New York and Jerusalem, 1996, p. 171.

12. How Should I Mark My Return to Judaism?

QUESTION

Dear Rabbi,

Both my mother and father's side of the family hid their Jewish roots out of fear. My mother's side began hiding their Judaism in the mid 1800s during the reformations in Germany, and my father's side began much earlier than that.

I recently found that some family members knew that we were of Jewish heritage, but did not tell other family members. I have cousins on my mother's side who are practicing Judaism and who say that they always knew, but my mother's mother never told any of us that her family and even her husband's family, my grandfather, are of Jewish heritage. I have found my mother's maternal line in the JewishGen databases as well. My father's paternal line is Levi, but they stopped practicing Judaism some time ago, and I cannot pinpoint when that was.

My parents and I have felt very strong ties to Judaism all of my life, and my mother even remembers asking her mother about it when she was a child. We have all always felt Jewish, if I may put it that way, and our "religious" beliefs are perfectly in line with Judaism, although until recently we never went to synagogue. I have been attending Torah study for a few weeks now.

My question is this: I wish to return and help my family return to actively practicing Judaism. Must I convert, or is our "history" sufficient to be considered already Jewish? Is there such an understanding of "returning"? What are the official positions on this? I get conflicting reports.

ANSWER

Your story is moving and I very much respect your desire to research your family tree and find out more about your Jewish ancestry. It would be interesting to understand at which point and why members of your family decided to hide the fact that they were Jewish.

With respect to your question, family "history" does not make somebody Jewish under Jewish Law. To be considered halakhically Jewish, a person should be either born of a Jewish mother (see *Kiddushin* 68b; *Even Ha'ezer* 8:5) or converted to Judaism.

It seems that you have good reasons to believe that your mother is Jewish, but you should find a way to prove it. This is why, for the moment, you should concentrate your research on your mother's side. Who was your maternal grandmother? Was she Jewish? Did she have a Jewish wedding? Was her mother Jewish? Try to find more about their history. You indicate that you found your mother's maternal line in the JewishGen database. If you are able to prove that your mother and grandmother are Jewish, then you too are Jewish. Of course you will have to be circumcised (if you are not already).

In principle, Jewish Law does not require a ceremony for return, because a Jew who converts to another religion remains a Jew. But as explained by Rabbi Moshe Isserles, the Rema, the rabbis did require some kind of ceremony even if it was not halakhically mandatory. This is what the Rema writes:

> An apostate who repents does not need to immerse [in the *mikveh*]; however according to the Sages, he should immerse [in the *mikveh*] and accept upon himself membership [in the Jewish people] before three [judges] (*Yoreh De'ah* 268:12 in the Rema).

Return ceremonies were created for the return of *Anusim* (people who were forced to convert). Such a ceremony, including circumcision and immersion in a *mikveh*, is described in a fifteenth-century responsum by Rabbi Solomon ben Simeon Duran (*Responsa of the Rashbash*, No. 89). He composed a special prayer for the occasion:

> Our God and God of our fathers, bring success to your servant [returnee's name supplied here] and bestow your grace upon him. Just as you have moved his heart to return in complete repentance before you, so may you plant in his heart love and fear of you. Open his heart to your Torah

and guide him in the path of your commandments that he may find grace in your eyes. So may it be, and let us say Amen.

Boaz Cohen and David Golinkin, two Conservative authorities, describe the history of ceremonies marking the return for Jewish apostates from the 8th to the 19th centuries.

Recently in Israel, a ceremony was also created for the *Falash Mura*, Ethiopians Jews converted to Christianity, who have returned to Israel and to Judaism.

If you cannot prove that your mother is Jewish and if you want to be recognized as a Jew according to Jewish Law, you will have no other choice but to go through the process of conversion. This could be a very positive experience, because the main part of the conversion process is learning and you have already begun to learn Torah. I think that you would enjoy it.

Best of luck,

Rabbi Monique Susskind Goldberg
November 2005

FOR FURTHER READING

1. Cohen, Boaz, "The Repentant Apostate" in David Golinkin, editor, *Proceedings of the Committee on Jewish Law and Standards of the Conservative Movement 1927-1970*, vol. 3, Jerusalem, 1997, pp. 1352-1354.

2. Golinkin, David, "How Can Apostates Such as the Falash Mura Return to Judaism?", http://www.schechter.edu/responsa.aspx?ID=30

3. *Moreh Derekh*, The Rabbinical Assembly Rabbi's Manual, edited by Perry Raphael Rank and Gordon M. Freeman, New York, 1998, vol. 2, pp. J-20-J-22.

4. Return ceremony proposal for *Anusim* (people who were forced to convert) from Schulamith Halevy: http://www.cs.tau.ac.il/~nachumd/sch/sch/anusim.html

5. Return process for *Falasha Mura* coming back to Israel and the Jewish people: http://www.ethiopianisraeliproject.org/pages/sample_interview.htm

6. Zelizer, Gerald, "Second Generation Apostates", *Responsa 1991-2000*, New York, 2002, pp. 146-150.

13. If I Convert, Do I Really Have to Keep 613 *Mitzvot?*

QUESTION

Dear Rabbi,

I read that in order to convert to Judaism, a convert must agree to adhere to all 613 *mitzvot* at the time of his conversion. Isn't this requirement a little unreasonable?

I've been studying Judaism for four years now, and if I were to convert, there is no way I would be able to say "yes, from this day forward I will follow all 613 *mitzvot*". In all honesty, I could commit to telling the rabbi I would try, but more than that would be impossible.

ANSWER

The Talmud says that when somebody wants to convert he/she is taught some of the "easier" *mitzvot* and some of the more "difficult" *mitzvot*, as well as their concomitant rewards and punishments (*Yevamot* 47a-b). This is how the major codes of Jewish law rule (see Maimonides, Laws of Forbidden Sexual Relations 14:2-4; Rabbi Joseph Karo, *Yoreh De'ah* 268:2).

According to one source (*Bekhorot* 30b), if the prospective convert rejects even one rabbinic rule, he/she is not accepted. This opinion was not followed in any code. Some authorities explain that if you accept in principle that all laws are binding, and you are aware that not observing them is considered a sin, you can be accepted into the fold and all transgressions are your sole responsibility (see for example Rabbi Ben-Zion Uziel, *Piskei Uziel B'she'elot Hazman*, No. 68).

By the way, it is impossible to observe 613 *mitzvot* today: For example, without the Temple, all laws concerning sacrifices and other Temple rituals aren't being practiced; anyone living outside the land of Israel cannot observe specific laws that apply only to inhabitants of the land; there are certain laws that apply only to specific groups, i.e. men, women, Levites or Kohanim; and finally, certain laws are applicable only under given circumstances. In total, I believe that only about one third of all the *mitzvot* can be observed today. (See R. Yisrael Meir HaKohen,

Sefer Hamitzvot Hakatzar, Jerusalem, 1990, who lists 271 *mitzvot* which can be observed today.)

As you can see, what is important is your commitment to the system of *mitzvot* and your sincere efforts to observe as many *mitzvot* as you can.

Sincerely,

Rabbi Diana Villa
February 2002

FOR FURTHER READING

1. Friedman, Tuvia, "A Responsum Regarding Halakhic Conversion" in David Golinkin, ed., *Be'er Tuvia*, Jerusalem, 1991, Hebrew section, pp. 31-40.

2. Golinkin, David, "Conflicting Approaches to Conversion in the United States in the Twentieth Century", *Conservative Judaism* 54/1 (Fall 2001), pp. 81-95.

3. *idem*, "A Responsum Regarding the Annulment of Conversions", http://www.schechter.edu/responsa. aspx?ID=23.

14. Is It Possible to Annul a Conversion?

QUESTION

Dear Rabbi,

I have undergone a Conservative and an Orthodox conversion. Since then, I've taken advanced Torah and Talmud classes at University. Although I believe in the Written Law, I very much question the Oral tradition. I also disagree with all this internal strife between the movements. I feel Judaism has not been a positive aspect in my life. It has separated me from friends, family and life experiences with no positive results.

In retrospect, if I had the information I have now, I would not have converted to any form of Judaism, rabbinic or not. Is there any possible way to legally annul my conversions, or at least the one that meant the most to me, the Conservative one? I want to have peace in my life, and although I will not convert to any other religion because of what I learned from Judaism, I am beginning to understand that I do not want to be Jewish.

ANSWER

I am sorry that Judaism has been such a negative experience for you. I imagine you must have had your reasons for converting and, assuming you had a year of studies before your original conversion and additional studies for your second conversion, you had ample time to evaluate the meaning and implications of your endeavor.

Although the movements differ in their respective approaches and interpretations, we are still all part of the Jewish people and have not splintered off into different religions. Jews still feel responsible for their brethren irrespective of their beliefs or practices.

A prospective convert is examined by Orthodox and Conservative Rabbinic Courts after a process that involves studying, circumcision for males and immersion. *The Ethics of the Fathers* begins with a statement which many commentators understand to refer to the transmission of the Oral law, which traditionally is considered part of the revelation on Mt. Sinai:

Moses received the Torah [i.e., both written and oral] from Sinai and transmitted it to Joshua, and Joshua to the Elders, and the Elders to the Prophets, and the Prophets to the men of the Great Synagogue (*Avot* 1:1).

Hence, Rabbinic Judaism includes both the Written and Oral Torah.

When the Talmud discusses the immersion of a convert, it says:

When he comes up after his ablution he is deemed to be an Israelite in all respects. In respect to what practical issue? In that if he retracted and then betrothed the daughter of an Israelite, he is regarded as a non-conforming Israelite and his betrothal is valid (*Yevamot* 47b).

On this basis, the codes rule that a convert who recants on his conversion is an apostate, yet his betrothal (as well as any other legal acts he performs) has the same legal validity as that of any other Jew (see *Yoreh De'ah* 268:2).

A convert cannot revert back to the status of a non-Jew. I would urge you to look into the many different expressions of Judaism available today and find one that is suitable to you.

Please let me know if I can answer further questions and/or refer you to a colleague in your area.

Sincerely,

Rabbi Diana Villa
April 2007

FOR FURTHER READING

Golinkin, David, "A Responsum Regarding the Annulment of Conversions", http://www.schechter.edu/responsa.aspx?ID=23.

15. What Is the Origin of the Conversion Rituals?

QUESTION

Dear Rabbi,

It is my understanding that the conversion rituals in use by most Jewish denominations today are products of Rabbinic Judaism and that such rituals, with the exception of circumcision, were not in practice during biblical times. In arguably the most famous biblical conversion, Ruth accepts Judaism through just a statement of affirmation to her mother-in-law Naomi.

My question is, why were these conversion rituals established by the Rabbis? Are they based on any scriptures in the Bible? Why does an affirmation of belief and devotion to the Jewish religion and people no longer suffice to become a Jew?

ANSWER

It seems that we cannot learn from Ruth's example about conversion in Biblical times since we do not know if such a concept existed. In the book of Ezra (Chapter 10) we are told that the non-Jewish women were separated from their Jewish husbands. Yet, we do not hear about the existence of an alternative, i.e., for them to convert to Judaism.

Since Biblical times, the time-frame of the story of Ruth, Jewish Law has developed, and more precise rules for conversion have been set. The conversion ritual as we know it today probably has its origin in the period after the destruction of the Second Temple (70 C.E). This ritual included circumcision for men, which as you said already existed in the Bible, and the immersion in the *mikveh*, the ritual bath. This is often explained symbolically as a new birth, i.e., the converted person is born anew into the Jewish people.

The primary difference between Ruth's "conversion" and conversion in accordance with *halakhah*, is that the Rabbis require that the candidate for conversion learns the basics of Jewish Law. It is no longer enough to claim "Your people will be my people, your God will be my God". In our time, Judaism is Rabbinic Judaism, and a person cannot enter Judaism without having a

46

basic knowledge of it (see *Yevamot* 47a-b; Maimonides, Laws of Forbidden Sexual Relations 14:1-3; *Yoreh De'ah* 268:2).

Today, therefore, conversion requires at least a few months of learning with a teacher if possible, and when the candidate for conversion is ready, a rabbinical court asks him/her if s/he accepts in principle the bulk of the *mitzvot* [commandments]. This does not mean that he/she is able to **practice** all 613 commandments (not every commandment can be observed, especially those that relate specifically to Temple ritual, and even among the other commandments, there are different levels of observance), but the Rabbinical court requests that the convert obligates him/herself to the entire **system** of *mitzvot*. Only after he/she accepts them can the convert perform the ritual acts of circumcision and *mikveh* (Maimonides and *Shulḥan Arukh, loc. cit.*).

Rabbi Monique Susskind Goldberg
February 2005

FOR FURTHER READING

1. Cohen, Shaye J.D., "Crossing the Boundaries and Becoming a Jew", in *The Beginnings of Jewishness: Boundaries, Varieties, Uncertainties*, Berkeley/Los Angeles/London, 1999, pp. 140 *ff.*

2. Sagi, Avi and Zohar, Tzvi, *Transforming Identity, The Ritual Transformation from Gentile to Jew*, New York, 2007, Part II: The *Giyyur* Ritual, pp. 105-218.

3. Samet, Moshe, "Conversion in the First Centuries C.E.", in *Jews and Judaism in the Second Temple, Mishna and Talmud Period: Studies in Honour of Shmuel Safrai*, edited by Isaiah Gafni, Aharon Oppenheimer, Menahem Stern, Jerusalem, 1993, pp. 316-343 [Hebrew].

ETHICS AND MORALITY

16. Does Jewish Law Permit Animal Experimentation?

QUESTION

Dear Rabbi,

What does Jewish law state regarding the ethics of animal experimentation for the advancement of medical research?

ANSWER

We read in the Torah that God gave men dominion over animals (Genesis 1:26). The rabbis also stated that animals were created to serve men (*Kiddushin* 82a) and that whatever is done to animals for man's benefit is permitted (see Rabbi Israel Isserlein, *Pesakim Uketavim*, No. 105).

This is why the authorities allow using animals for medicine and other human needs and there is no prohibition due to *tza'ar ba'alei ḥayyim* [the prohibition of causing suffering to animals] (see the Rema in his gloss to *Even Ha'ezer* 5:14). On this basis, modern Jewish decisors have ruled that experimentation on animals is permitted, whether or not immediate results are apparent, and it is definitely allowed by Jewish Law to test medicine on animals to make sure it is not harmful to human beings. The authorities also allow the use of animals for experimentation, research and diagnostic purposes (see Rabbi Eliezer Waldenberg, *Tzitz Eliezer* vol. 14, No. 68).

However, *tza'ar ba'alei ḥayyim* is an important principle in Jewish law (see *Bava Metzi'a* 32b-33a; Maimonides, Laws of Murder and the Preservation of Life 13:13; *Ḥoshen Mishpat* 272:9). This is why, even if *tza'ar ba'alei ḥayyim* is sometimes overuled by the use of animals for men's needs, unnecessary cruelty to animals should definitely be avoided (see for example the Rema on *Ḥoshen Mishpat, ibid.*)

Sincerely,

Rabbi Diana Villa
May 2005

FOR FURTHER READING

1. Abrams, Judith and Steven, "The Use of Animals in Research", in: "Walter Jacob and Moshe Zemer, eds., *The Fetus and Fertility in Jewish Law: Essays and Responsa*, Pittsburgh and Tel Aviv, 1995, pp. 119-130.

2. Bleich, J. David, "Judaism and Animal Experimentation", *Tradition* 22/1 (Spring 1986), pp. 1-36 = *Contemporary Halakhic Problems*, vol. III, New York, 1989, chapter IX.

3. Cohen, Alfred, "Animal Experimentation", *Journal of Halacha and Contemporary Society* XI (Spring 1986), pp. 19-32.

4. Steinberg, Avraham, "Medical Experiments on Animals" *Sefer Asia* 1, Jerusalem, 1979, pp. 263-269 [Hebrew].

5. *idem*, "Cruelty to Animals", *Encyclopedia of Jewish Medical Ethics*, vol. 1, Jerusalem-New York, 2003, pp. 258-271.

17. May I Keep an Item That Was Sent to Me by Mistake?

QUESTION

Dear Rabbi,

The Federal Trade Commission says it's perfectly legal to keep an item that was mailed to you if you didn't order it. I recently ordered a computer hard drive for $500 from a major company. The company sent me two of them. The packing slip says only one was shipped. I really want to keep the extra hard drive. What should I do and why?

ANSWER

I am not familiar with the Federal Trade Commission's rules, but the fact that something is legal does not mean that it is ethical, and it certainly does not mean that it is in accordance with Jewish Law.

In my opinion, keeping the second hard drive that was sent to you by mistake is taking something that does not belong to you. You are taking advantage of the sender's mistake. In other words, it is a lack of honesty. Leviticus 5:23 states: "... He shall restore that which he took by robbery... or the lost thing which he found". See also *Ḥoshen Mishpat*, 232:1, which explicitly notes that if there was a mistake in a transaction, and too much or too little was given, one has to return the difference even if a few years have passed.

Another point to take into consideration is that even though it is probable that companies take into account these kinds of losses, and would not act to retrieve their item, there is a Talmudic principle that one should act *lifnim mishurat hadin*, beyond the strict letter of the law (see for instance *Bava Metzi'a* 24b and elsewhere).

Ḥoshen Mishpat 259:5 describes a situation where a person found an object, and in the case in question, was not obligated by law to return it to the owner. However, Rabbi Joseph Karo (author of the *Shulḥan Arukh*) writes: "it's good and right to act beyond the strict word of the law, and to give back the found object".

In conclusion, I believe that according to *halakhah* you should return the extra hard drive to its owner and that, as Jews, we should serve as models of moral behavior.

Rabbi Monique Susskind Goldberg
July 2007

FOR FURTHER READING

1. Amsel, Nachum, *The Jewish Encyclopedia of Moral and Ethical Issues*, Northvale, New Jersey and London, 1996, pp. 29-33, 327-329.
2. Moriel, Yehudah, *B'derekh Tovim*, Jerusalem, 1985, pp. 38-44 [Hebrew].

18. Does Ritual Observance Take Precedence Over Parental Respect?

QUESTION

Dear Rabbi,

I have recently become strictly observant, as far as following the rules of Shabbat, *kashrut* and ritual observance in general. My mother is a secular Jew who feels a strong Jewish identification, but after the Holocaust my family grew more hostile towards Judaism. They have never been observant and are bothered by my increased observance of *halakhah*.

Now, the only place where I still eat vegetarian food from non-kosher utensils and pots and pans, is in my mother's house. I try to *kasher* individual utensils from time to time, but this cannot be done with the dishware. I feel in a double-bind: yes, I am violating *halakhah* when eating in her kitchen but, on the other hand, insisting that I keep separate utensils and pans would be an affront to her. She frequently voices her discontent with my level of observance and I know she is very bitter towards the Jewish community in general. I am trying to balance two realities: the halakhic reality and the reality of *kibud em* [respect for one's mother]. How can I honor my mother whilst also staying true to the Jewish dietary laws? The whole situation is so emotionally precarious.

Does ritual observance take precedence over family unity? What is your advice?

ANSWER

Honoring one's parents is one of the Ten Commandments (see Exodus 20:11 and Deuteronomy 5:15) and revering one's parents is another *mitzvah* (Leviticus 19:3). The Talmud describes in detail what honoring and revering parents entails (for example: supplying all his/her needs, not sitting in a parent's place, not contradicting him/her; see *Kiddushin* 30b-32a and *Yoreh De'ah*, paragraphs 240-241). Yet that respect has its limits. If a parent is annoyed by the fact that one is observant, one cannot really accommodate him/her. One cannot obey one's parents if they order one to transgress a *mitzvah*. The Talmud (*Yevamot* 6a) says that if the father asks his son who is a Kohen to break the laws of purity or not to return a lost object, he cannot obey his father, as God's honor comes before the parents' honor. According to Rabbi Joseph Karo (*Yoreh De'ah* 240:15), one cannot disobey even a rabbinic law if a parent requests it.

As far as revering your mother without transgressing *kashrut* laws, we suggest the following.

According to Jewish dietary laws, you can eat cold uncooked foods in your mother's home, such as fruits and vegetables. Some other foods are possible as well:

1. Bread (as long as it is clear that it has no non-kosher ingredients such as lard, see below. No. 47).

2. Cheeses (even without a *hekhsher* or rabbinic stamp of approval, for those who accept the opinion that rennet from animals that are not slaughtered according to Jewish law is permitted – see below, No. 40).

3. Canned sardines.

4. Canned tuna (preferably with a *hekhsher*, since some authorities are wary that non-kosher fish may be mixed with the tuna fish in the can).

5. Smoked salmon.

6. Pickled herring (preferably kosher, since there are some special considerations regarding pickled products in Jewish law).

You can also have a stock of kosher products in your mother's home, including crackers, cookies, gefilte fish jars, etc., to make it easier when you visit your mother. (For more details about *kashrut*, see Samuel Dresner, Seymour Siegel and David Pollock, *Keeping Kosher: A Diet for the Soul*, New York, 2000, pp. 50-67.)

It is obvious that you are trying to make the best of a very difficult situation, so keep trying to use kosher dishes, pots and pans, and try to observe as much as you possibly can according to Jewish law. Nowadays, disposable pans, dishes and cutlery are also available.

It is best to avoid conflict as much as you possibly can. You clearly respect your mother and let us hope that she will learn to respect your way of life.

Sincerely,

Rabbi Diana Villa
March 2005

FOR FURTHER READING

1. Blidstein, Gerald, *Honor Thy Father and Mother*, New York, 1975, pp. 80-94.

2. Yosef, Yitzhak, *Sefer Yalkut Yosef: Hilkhot Kibbud Av Va'em*, Jerusalem, 5761, Chapters 7, 9, 11 [Hebrew].

19. An Embarrassing Question

QUESTION

Dear Rabbi,

I come to you with a very embarrassing question. I ask you please not to judge or condemn me for asking, and I hope you won't be offended.

I'm a young, unmarried man. I have met my soul-mate, and, God willing, we will get married some day, and have a wonderful life together as husband and wife. I want to be her husband in every way, take care of her, shower her with love and intimacy, and give her a good home and a family.
BUT I'm not married yet. Sometimes (well, a LOT of times) I masturbate. To me, masturbation is very pleasurable, and I enjoy it very much. But I am worried; is it really permitted? I have told my girlfriend (future wife, I hope) about it, and she has no problem with it, but – like me – she felt uncertain if it's a sin or not. The problem is that I enjoy masturbation so much, that I might want to masturbate sometimes even when I'm married! Would that be permitted?

Rabbi, I know you must be shocked and disgusted. I'm really not a pervert. I try to be a good man, I love God and His Torah, I am a good friend, a family-oriented person, a hard worker. My question is: what should I do? Is this permitted or is it sinful/ evil?

ANSWER

I am not here to judge you and certainly not to condemn you. Here is what I can tell you:

1. The *halakhah* is clear. Male masturbation should be avoided in order not to spill seed. See, for instance, *Even Ha'ezer* 23:42.

2. Love between husband and wife is natural and sacred. See, for example, Genesis 2:24: "Therefore shall a man leave his father and his mother, and shall cleave unto his wife, and they shall be one flesh".

58

3. According to *halakhah*, a husband is obligated to satisfy his wife sexually. Maimonides (Laws of Marriage 12:2) includes sexual relations among the ten obligations a married man has to his wife (see also *Even Ha'ezer* 69:2).

With those points in mind, you must make your own decisions. I believe that once you are married, you will be able and happy to focus on your wife, and you will not need other solitary satisfactions.

Perhaps you should find a local Rabbi with whom you could discuss your doubts. However, I am open to answer more of your questions.

Rabbi Monique Susskind Goldberg
July 2006

FOR FURTHER READING

1. Epstein, Louis, *Sex Laws and Customs in Judaism*, New York, 1948, 1967, pp. 146-147.

2. Feldman, David M., *Birth Control in Jewish Law*, third edition, [Jerusalem], 1995, Chapter 6.

3. Gold, Michael, *Does God Belong in the Bedroom?*, Philadelphia and Jerusalem, 1992, pp. 175-178.

20. Is Cat Spaying Allowed by Jewish Law?

QUESTION

Dear Rabbi,

Is it permissible to spay a female cat by removing her ovaries? If so, under what circumstances?

ANSWER

In Leviticus 22:24 we read: "You shall not offer unto the Lord that which is bruised or crushed or broken or cut". The Sages understood that the verse is referring to animals with damaged sexual organs. They deduced from this verse that not only is it forbidden to offer a sterilized animal as a sacrifice, but also that to sterilize animals (and humans) in general, is a biblical prohibition (see *Sifra Emor* 7:11; *Bekhorot* 33b and elsewhere).

However, when they state the law, the authorities point to the fact that the interdiction deals only with sterilizing **male** animals. There is even an opinion that the act of sterilization [*seirus*] does not apply to female animals because the Biblical verse refers to damaging external organs (*Sifra Emor* 7:12). This may be the reason why, according to Maimonides (Laws of Forbidden Sexual Relations 16:11) and the *Shulḥan Arukh* (*Even Ha'ezer* 5:11), the law is different for a male and for a female. Although it is forbidden to sterilize a female (human or animal), if one does it, there is no punishment incurred for this act. The *Shulḥan Arukh* (*ibid.* 5:12) even permits sterilization of females by way of medication as opposed to through invasive procedures which cause physical damage to the sexual organs (see also *Responsa Bemar'eh Habazak*, vol. 6, No. 77).

There is also an opinion that allows a non-Jew to neuter the animals (see R. Shlomo Kluger, *Ha'elef Lekha Shlomo, Even Ha'ezer* No. 23; R. Shmuel Wosner, *Shevet Halevi*, vol. 6, No. 204). Rabbi Shlomo Aviner even allows a Jewish veterinarian to spay female pets (see *She'eilat Shlomo* v. 6).

Another consideration that enters the discussion about spaying a female cat is the halakhic injunction against cruelty to animals (*tza'ar ba'alei ḥayyim*; see *Bava Metzi'a* 32a; Maimonides, Laws of Murder and the Preservation of Life 13:13; *Ḥoshen Mishpat* 272:9 in the Rema).

Animal activists agree that cats should be sterilized for their own well-being for the following reasons:

1. A female cat is in heat from January to August and can, if let free, give birth every three months to three to eight kittens. It's obvious that there is no way the cat can take care of so many kittens and they frequently die of starvation and sickness.

2. If a female does not mate and repeatedly goes into heat, there is a danger of life-threatening uterine infections and uterine and ovarian cancer.

3. Spaying also reduces the risk of mammary cancer.

4. Males that are not neutered can become aggressive toward their owners, and will get into fights with other males as they search for females. The frequent fights expose them to infectious diseases and abscesses from wounds.

For these reasons and in order to avoid the killing of thousands of roaming cats and dogs, the Israeli Knesset recently passed a law promoting the reduction of births in cats and dogs (Law Against Cruelty to Animals 2008).

Rabbi Shlomo Brody, in a recent responsum on our subject, mentioned that Chief Sephardic Rabbi Shlomo Amar has expressed the view that because of the public safety concerns from wild and ownerless animals, one may ask a non-Jewish veterinarian to neuter pets of both genders.

In conclusion, although sterilizing animals (as well as humans) is in principle forbidden by Jewish Law, there are grounds to allow sterilizing a cat, especially a female cat, because of the halakhic injunction of avoiding cruelty to animals (*tza'ar ba'alei ḥayyim*).

Sterilization through medication would be completely acceptable from a halakhic point of view and would be better than spaying. However, although chemical contraception for cats exists (in two forms, tablets and injections), as far as I can see from my reading, they are not 100% effective. So, on that point, you should consult with your veterinarian.

If possible, it is better to have the spaying done by a non-Jewish veterinarian.

Rabbi Monique Susskind Goldberg
March 2006 and July 2008

FOR FURTHER READING

1. Brody, Shlomo, "Neutering Animals", *Up Front, The Jerusalem Post*, 14 May 2009, p. 41, also available at www.jpost.com.

2. Chemical contraception for cats: www.isabellevets.co.uk/ health_advice/cat/info/birthcontrolcat.htm

3. The Importance of Sterilizing Cats, www.ezinearticles.com/ ?The-Importance-of-Sterilizing-Cats!&id=1295028 - 46k

4. Israeli Law Against Cruelty to Animals (Amendment No. 7) 2008. http://www.knesset.gov.il/Laws/heb/template.asp?type=1

21. Isn't *Sheḥitah* Cruelty to Animals?

QUESTION

Dear Rabbi,

I was raised in a Jewish home and was taught that mercy and kindness towards animals was one of the most sacred Jewish laws. My mother and father however, prepared meals containing meat and dairy, and they never once taught us about the practices required to slaughter animals for food. I have spent much time reading about kosher and conventional slaughter. One would be in grave denial assuming that animals did not experience horrific stress and agony from either method.

It seems a grave conflict in Jewish doctrine to teach children empathy for animals yet ignore their pain and suffering so that they can provide food neither required nor healthy in the human diet.

It seems to me that within any truly intelligent religion that takes the holistic view of its laws in the context of modernity, the slaughtering of billions of animals can be nothing more than a wedge between the truly holy and merciful practice of faith, and a practice that keeps us from progressing beyond much of the violence we are experiencing today. I read emails every day about the pandemic of animal abuse because we so readily accept that their prime reason for life is death for food. It is wrong and we are ignoring the bigger picture that I believe we are obligated to see.

What of the human beings who work all day killing animals; how can this manifest into a positive energy in the world? I believe our worst mistake, our most profound and tragic sin is that of killing animals for food. Perhaps it was necessary for survival once, but today, it is keeping us in a violent and inhumane cycle.

Author Isaac Bashevis Singer wrote: "In relation to animals, all people are Nazis, for them it is eternal Treblinka". I believe that the reality of slaughterhouses justifies this comparison. The cruelty involved with eating meat is contrary to Jewish law.

ANSWER

First of all, let me tell you that I empathize with a lot of your arguments, and I do believe that we should all protest against cruel behavior toward animals. This is true especially for the Jewish religious leadership because, as you rightly state, mercy and kindness to animals is an essential commandment in Jewish Law.

This being said, one must face reality: humanity is not ready to accept giving up eating meat. This was the reality already described in the book of Genesis, and this is still the reality today.

In the beginning of creation, God meant for mankind to be vegetarian. We read in Genesis (1:29):

> God said: See I give you every seed-bearing plant that is upon all the earth, and every tree that has seed-bearing fruit; they shall be yours for food.

God expected people not to kill living creatures for their food, but after the flood, God realized that man had an urge to eat meat (Deuteronomy 12:20). So God accepted a compromise – man may eat animals, but in order to remind him that life is a supreme value, man is forbidden to eat the meat with the blood (see Genesis 9:3-4). This is how *Shehitah*, the kosher way of slaughtering animals by cutting the jugular artery and draining the blood (*Yoreh De'ah* 20:1-4; 28:1) came into being.

Joseph Telushkin has an interesting insight about *Shehitah*. He writes:

> The unique practice of draining blood from meat consumed by Jews has had over thousands of years a profoundly moral impact. It has helped produce an extraordinary antipathy to bloodthirst.

Jewish Law is aware of man's weakness and desire for meat, but at the same time, tries to limit the pain and suffering to animals. *Shehitah* is intended to avoid animal suffering, and scientific opinion corroborates that it is the most humane method of slaughter. There is one kosher slaughterhouse in the U.S. that has been documented as having inhumane practices, because of the way the animals are shackled and hoisted. The Committee of Jewish Law and Standards of the Rabbinical Assembly (Conservative) has condemned this practice, which is against the 1958 Humane Slaughter Act.

There is also a tendency in Jewish sources to diminish the amount of meat consumed by permitting the consumption of only certain animals (see Leviticus, Chapter 11).

The reality being what it is, my belief is that we Jews together with others have to fight with all our strength and power against abuse and cruelty to animals. We should support the idea of *"hekhsher tzedek"* promoted by the Conservative Movement. Its principle can be summarized as whatever is kosher should also be ethical. This includes strict rules for slaughterhouses and fighting for better conditions for raising animals. Consumers can, for example, eat only eggs from free-range chickens and request a clear knowledge of the conditions in which animals intended for consumption are raised and slaughtered. We should also try to reduce the amount of meat consumed, which would be kinder to animals, and better for our health and for the economy of food production on earth. We should also avoid eating veal raised in factory farms.

But, there is one argument that you cannot use in your righteous fight, especially not if you want the Jewish leadership on your side. I am referring to the comparison with the Nazis killing the Jews in the concentration camps. I have seen the pictures used by animal activists comparing animals in slaughterhouses and inmates in concentration camps. Those pictures are repulsive and do not serve your cause. This comparison is morally wrong. There is nothing equal to the horror of Treblinka and Auschwitz. Please respect the memory of the millions of our brothers and sisters who were murdered by the Nazis.

Rabbi Monique Susskind Goldberg
April 2003

FOR FURTHER READING

1. Dorff, Elliot N. and Roth, Joel, "Shackling and Hoisting", *Responsa 1991-2000*, New York, 2002, pp. 93-97. Also available at: http://www.grandin.com/riyual/conservative.jewish.Law.html

2. Dresner, Samuel *et al*, *Keeping Kosher: A Diet for the Soul*, New York, 2000, pp. 16-17.

3. Ginzberg, Louis, *The Responsa of Professor Louis Ginzberg*, edited by David Golinkin, New York and Jerusalem, 1996, pp. 146-150.

4. Golinkin, David, "The Kashrut of Veal", *Responsa in a Moment*, Jerusalem, 2000, pp. 73-77.

5. Klein, Isaac, "*Sheḥitah*", in *A Guide to Jewish Religious Practice*, New York, 1992, pp. 307-310.

6. Steinberg, Avraham, "Cruelty to Animals", *Encyclopedia of Jewish Medical Ethics*, vol. 1, Jerusalem-New York, 2003, pp. 258-271.

7. Telushkin, Joseph, "Prevention of Cruelty to Animals / *Tza'ar Ba'alei Ḥayyim*", in: *Jewish Literacy, The Most Important Things to Know About the Jewish Religion, Its People, and Its History*, New York, 1991, p. 578.

22. Should We Fire Illegal Foreign Workers?

QUESTION

Dear Rabbi,

My wife and I have contracted for several years with a foreign-born gardener and a foreign-born family housekeeping crew (both of which come once per week). They work hard and we are happy with their services. I very strongly suspect, however, that they are in this country illegally. I am wondering what my halakhic responsibilities are regarding continuing to use their services.

On the one hand, it seems obvious that using the services of illegal workers – if they are illegal – is wrong. I am facilitating their presence here. I am taking work away from higher-priced, legal competitors, who comply with the laws, provide workers' compensation insurance, etc.

On the other hand, firing these individuals would suddenly penalize them after several years of good service.

I do not know for a fact that they are in this country illegally, and if I ask for proof, they might be insulted (if they are legal) or provide me false documents (if they are not).

To complicate matters even further, my wife is employed by a local public school district and teaches English to foreign born adults, nearly all of whom are here illegally. The District's policy is "don't ask, don't tell". My wife sees little difference between teaching the illegals in her school and continuing to hire them at home. She is already upset over the fact that I am even considering firing our cleaner and gardener.

What are my halakhic obligations and priorities?

ANSWER

You are in a difficult situation, and before taking a decision, you should try to find out if the workers in question are indeed in your country illegally.

I do not think your wife's teaching can be compared to your hiring. As I understand it, it is not against the law to teach, but it is against the law to hire illegal workers. As painful as it may be, if you find out that they live illegally in your country, as a Jew who keeps *mitzvot*, it is not befitting that you act against the laws of your country. The *halakhah* states: *dina demalkhuta dina* – "the law of the land is the law" (see, for example, *Bava Kama* 113a; *Yoreh De'ah* 165:1 in the Rema, and elsewhere) which means that you have to respect the law of the country you live in.

Perhaps there is a way you can help these workers to become legal?

Rabbi Monique Susskind Goldberg
June 2008

FOR FURTHER READING

Encyclopaedia Judaica, second edition, Jerusalem, 2007, "Dina De-Malkhuta Dina", vol. 5, pp. 663-669.

23. Who Has Priority in Entering a Bomb Shelter During a Rocket Attack?

QUESTION

Dear Rabbi,

I live in Sderot. During the rocket attacks, we have to enter a public shelter and sometimes there is not sufficient space to accommodate everybody. According to which criteria should we decide who enters the shelter?

ANSWER

Your question is very difficult to answer. Rather than offer you a definitive answer, I will provide you with several approaches in *halakhah* about this issue.

Saving of life is an ultimate value in Judaism. As we read in the *Mishnah* in *Sanhedrin* (4:5): "Whoever saves a life, Scripture considers him as if he had saved the entire world".[1] Saving a life is even more important that keeping Shabbat and most of the other commandments (see, for example, *Oraḥ Ḥayyim* 329:1).

In this context, many halakhic authorities have pondered over the question of how much one can endanger his/her own life for the sake of saving another person's life. Here is a summary of the main opinions on the subject:

1. On the one hand, it is a *mitzvah* for a Jew to save the life of another person.

This opinion is based on the Biblical verse "You shall not stand idly by the blood of your neighbour" (Leviticus 19:16).

This approach is found in the Talmud, where we read:

> Whence do we know that if a man sees his companion drowning, or being mauled by a wild beast, or attacked by

---

1   There are different versions of this sentence and in our standard Mishnah editions we have: "Whoever saves the life *of a Jew*". But in many manuscripts of the Talmud the word "of a Jew" does not appear and this is the original version. See E.E. Uhrbach, *The World of the Sages*, Jerusalem, 1988, pp. 561-577 [Hebrew].

bandits, that he is obliged to save him? The Bible says: "You shall not stand idly by the blood of your neighbour" (*Sanhedrin* 73a).

From this Talmudic passage we can conclude that it is a commandment to help save a person in a life-threatening situation and this was codified as *halakhah* (see Maimonides, Book of the Commandments, Negative Commandments 297; Laws of Murder and the Preservation of Life 1:14-16; *Ḥoshen Mishpat* 426:1).

2. On the other hand, it is forbidden for a Jew to put himself in obvious danger even for the sake of saving another Jew. As it is written: "Do not bring blood upon your house" (see Deut. 22:8), and "Protect yourself and keep your soul (from danger)" (*ibid.* 4:9).

In other words, one does not reject one soul for the sake of another soul [*ein doḥin nefesh mipnei nefesh*] (*Sanhedrin* 72b).

In the Babylonian Talmud (*Sanhedrin* 74a), we are told that a certain man came to Rava and said: "The governor of my town has ordered me to go and kill so-and-so, saying: if you do not kill him, I will kill you". Rava answered, "Let him rather kill you, but you may not kill the other man. Who can say that your blood is redder than his? Perhaps his blood is redder than yours".

Following the same principle, one cannot say to someone "sacrifice your life to save another person", because who can say that your neighbour's blood is redder than yours? The life of one person cannot be valued more or less than the life of another person, and there is thus no commandment to get killed for the sake of saving another person. On this subject, Maimonides insists that a person should not put himself in any danger (*ibid.* 11:4-5).

R. Eliezer Waldenberg, a well-known contemporary halakhic authority, states that one is not allowed to actively put oneself in danger for the sake of saving another person. He based himself on the talmudic passage in *Sanhedrin* 74a that we saw above and on another passage in *Niddah* 61a (see below and see *Responsa Tzitz Eliezer*, vol. 15, No. 70).

3. The halakhic authorities are divided on the question whether one can put oneself in **doubtful** danger for the sake of saving another person from **certain** danger. Here are the different opinions:

a) One is required to put oneself in **doubtful** danger in order to save another person from **certain** danger.

In the Jerusalem Talmud (*Terumot* 8:4, 46b) there is a discussion between Rabbi Yoḥanan and Resh Lakish about endangering themselves to save their friend, Rabbi Ami, who was attacked by thieves. R. Yoḥanan thought there was nothing to do because he could not endanger his own life to save his friend. Resh Lakish wanted to try and save R. Ami, even if by doing so he put himself in danger. The Talmud does not give a clear-cut decision on this.

The author of *Hagahot Maimoniot* (R. Meir HaKohen of Rothenburg) rules on the basis of this passage in the Jerusalem Talmud, that the *halakhah* is according to Resh Lakish and that one is obliged to put oneself in doubtful danger in order to save others from an obvious danger (quoted by R. Joseph Karo in *Kesef Mishneh* on Maimonides, Laws of Murder and the Preservation of Life 1:14 and in *Beit Yosef, Ḥoshen Mishpat* 426).

b) One is allowed but not required to put oneself in doubtful danger in order to save another person.

In the Talmud (*Niddah* 61a-b), we are told that R. Tarfon did not want to put himself even in doubtful danger in order to save people who were suspected of murder. It seems that the conclusion of the Talmud there is that one is not obliged to endanger oneself in order to save another person, even if the danger one risks is doubtful (see also *Ketubot* 61a-b and *Tosafot* on *Niddah* 61a, *s.v. atamrinkhu*)

Accordingly, some halakhic authorities rule that there is no obligation to endanger oneself for the sake of saving another person, even if the danger is doubtful. However one may do so and it is considered a *Midat Ḥasidut* [an act of piety] by some (see *Responsa Ha'amek She-eilah* 147:4; 159:4; *Shulḥan Arukh Harav, Oraḥ Ḥayyim* 329:8).

c) Other authorities consider it forbidden to take even a doubtful risk for the sake of saving another person. According to the Radbaz, it is foolish to take even doubtful risks to save another person (see, for example, *Responsa* of the *Radbaz*, vol. 3, No. 627).

In conclusion, from these sources we learn that, on the one hand, one is obliged, according to *halakhah*, to do the utmost to save life; but, on the other hand, it is forbidden to sacrifice one's own life to save another person's life.

When the danger one risks is doubtful, some authorities believe that one is obliged to take that risk in order to save others from certain danger. Other decisors state that there is no obligation to take any risk to save others, while others believe that it is forbidden by *halakhah* to take even a doubtful risk to save others, even from certain death.

A last point to take into account is that, according to some authorities, we should distinguish between dangers in times of peace and dangers in wartime where all the rules change (see for instance Rabbi Abraham Isaac Kuk in *Responsa Mishpat Kohen*, No. 143). In time of war, there is an opinion that one must endanger oneself to save others even from doubtful danger and even if they are not in the battlefield (see *Responsa Tzitz Eliezer*, vol. 12, No. 57; vol. 13, No. 100). Although rockets landing are clearly an attack, it is not clear whether the situation in Sderot and similar occurrences in other cities is to be considered in the context of wartime or not.

Applying these principles to your question, we see that according to *halakhah*, there is no clear criterion to decide who has priority to enter the shelter. "One does not reject one soul for the sake of another soul", because the blood of one person is not redder that the blood of another. However, one is required to save as many people as possible.

The fact that the rocket attacks on cities in general and on Sderot in particular, could be considered as being part of a war against the State of Israel and also the fact that Israeli soldiers are risking their life for the sake of protecting civilians, show that there is place for applying the principle that "all of Israel is responsible for one another" (*Shevuot* 39a). We should conclude, therefore, that people should take some kind of risk in order to save others (following in this the opinion of R. Joseph Karo who accepted the decision stated in *Hagahot Maimoniot*).

Logically, therefore, it seems to me that weaker members of the community (children, old, sick, and their helpers) should have priority in entering the shelter, with the hope that stronger and healthier people will find other safe shelters against the rockets. This seems to reflect the accepted community moral standards and it is the custom for sinking boats ("women and children first").

We pray to God that very soon we will be able to live in tranquility in our land and in peace with our neighbours, and that we will no longer have to deal with these kinds of questions.

Rabbi Monique Susskind Goldberg
January 2007

FOR FURTHER READING

1. Bleich, J. David, "Sacrificing the Few to Save the Many", *Tradition* 43/1 (Spring 2010), pp. 78-86.

2. Navon, Ya'akov, "Risking Lives to Save Lives", *Teḥumin* 4 (1983), pp. 153-172 [Hebrew].

3. Oshry, Ephraim, *She'eilot u-Teshuvot mi-Ma'amakim*, 5 volumes, New York, 1959-1974 [Hebrew] (cf. an English abbreviated edition, *Responsa from the Holocaust*, New York, 1983) dealt with similar topics. For our specific topic, see: http://www1.yadvashem.org/about_holocaust/documents/part3/doc182.html.

4. Za'afrani, Shmuel, "Putting Onself in Danger In Order to Save Lives", *Teḥumin* 19 (1999), pp. 91-94 [Hebrew].

GENDER

24. What is the Halakhic Status of a Transgender?

QUESTION

Dear Rabbi,

I have a long history of trying to deal with what was eventually diagnosed as Gender Identity Disorder. During the years I was struggling with my identity, I was under psychiatric treatment, including drugs and various forms of therapy, and attempted suicide a few times. As an observant Jew, I struggle with questions related to a sex change operation from male to female:

1. Is a person still Jewish after the operation?

2. Considering the high risk of suicide in people with this diagnosis, could the operation be allowed according to Jewish Law on the basis of *pikuah nefesh* [saving a life]?

3. What is the person's sex according to Jewish law after the operation? Can this woman marry a man?

4. Are there limitations to Jewish observance and synagogue membership? Is there any halakhic reason to treat that person any differently than a genetic woman?

ANSWER

1. In principle, Jewish law does not allow any mutilation of sexual organs. This would be a violation of the castration prohibition (see *Even Ha'ezer*, paragraph 5 and above, No. 20). However, a person who undergoes an operation to change his/her gender does not lose his/her Jewish status, does not need to convert and if he/she was a convert he/she remains Jewish.

2. If a competent medical authority certifies as to your Gender Identity Disorder diagnosis and that not doing the surgery would be potentially life-threatening to you, Jewish law would allow the operation, since *pikuah nefesh* [saving a life] overrides every commandment except for the prohibitions of murder, idolatry and sexual immorality (see *Yoma* 85b; *Sanhedrin* 74a and *Yoreh De'ah* 157:1). This is based on the principle in

Leviticus 18:5 "And he shall live by them" – the Sages were more concerned with health and life than with the transgression of any law (except the three we mentioned above). A law may even be transgressed to preserve mental health, like an abortion to avoid severe psychological suffering. (See Rabbi Eliezer Waldenberg on abortion, *Tzitz Eliezer*, vol. 13, No. 102.)

3. Regarding gender after the operation, the vast majority of decisors believe that the original gender is retained (the person is not a woman but a castrated man) even after the operation, notwithstanding the physical changes and the new sexual organs because, genetically, the person is still male (see for example, *Responsa Yaskil Avdi*, vol. 7, *Even Ha'ezer*, No. 4; for a comprehensive list of opinions, see *Entziklopedia Hilkhatit-Refu'it*, edited by Dr. Avraham Steinberg, vol. 4, p. 611, note 79), and therefore it would not be possible to marry a man. Some decisors follow the opinion that the external organs define gender. This is a minority opinion represented by Rabbi Mayer Rabinowitz who considers that surgical procedures and hormone treatments used today bring about a complete sex change that would be the basis to allow such marriages.

4. There is certainly no halakhic problem regarding synagogue membership and no reason to treat the person in question differently than any other member; however, there may be synagogue policies that determine how particular communities deal with these questions.

We hope that your decisions are such that you can live a long and fulfilling life, balancing your gender identity needs with the deep commitment to Torah and *mitzvot* we sense from your e-mail.

Sincerely,

Rabbi Diana Villa
May 2005

FOR FURTHER READING

1. Bleich, J. David, *Contemporary Halakhic Problems*, Vol. 1, New York and Hoboken, 1977, pp. 100-105.

2. Hadaya, Ovadiah, *Responsa Yaskil Avdi*, vol. 7, *Even Ha'ezer*, No. 4 [Hebrew].

3. Plaut, Gunther and Mark Washofsky, *Teshuvot for the Nineties*, New York, 1997, pp. 191-196.

4. Rabinowitz, Mayer, "Status of Transexuals", Committee on Jewish Law and Standards, 2003. Also available at: http://www.rabbinicalassembly.org/teshuvot/docs/20012004/rabinowitz_transsexuals.pdf.

5. Steinberg, Avraham, *Entziklopedia Hilkhatit-Refuit*, vol. 4, cols. 609-612 [Hebrew].

6. Waldenberg, Eliezer, *Tzitz Eliezer*, part 10, No. 25, chapter 26, section 6, pp. 167-169; part 11, No. 78; part 22, No. 2 [Hebrew].

INTERFAITH ISSUES

25. May Jewish Identity be Determined by DNA Tests?

QUESTION

Dear Rabbi,

My mother recently took a DNA test, showing results of a genetic marker that is found in Ashkenazic Jews and only Ashkenazic Jews.

However, I was not raised Jewish, she was not raised Jewish, and we are unaware of the identities of any Jewish ancestors. Am I Jewish?

ANSWER

The genetic marker you are referring to, found primarily in Ashkenazic Jews, is probably the gene for Tay-Sachs disease, a fatal genetic disorder that causes progressive destruction of the central nervous system in children.

> In the general population, about one out of every 320,000 babies born has Tay-Sachs disease and approximately one in 30 Ashkenazi Jews is a carrier of the gene that causes this disease. Even though there is a high incidence of this disease among people of Eastern European and Askhenazi Jewish descent, Tay-Sachs disease has been reported in children of virtually all ethnic, racial, and religious populations. French Canadians of the eastern St. Lawrence River Valley area of Quebec, Cajuns from Louisiana, and the Old Order Amish in Pennsylvania have been found to carry the mutation with frequencies equal to or even greater than those seen in the Ashkenazi Jewish population (see the website listed below).

Tay-Sachs disease is very serious, and in Israel, the doctors recommend that newlywed Ashkenazic Jews take a test to verify if they carry this gene. The risk of having a sick child exists only if both parents carry the gene.

As you can see from the quotation above, it is true that the genetic markers for Tay-Sachs disease are found with great frequency in Ashkenazic Jews, but they are not unique to

Ashkenazic Jews. Accordingly, finding a genetic marker common among Ashkenazic Jews in your DNA does not make you Jewish.

Traditionally, Jewish law defines a Jew as someone who has a Jewish mother, or someone who converted to Judaism (see *Kiddushin* 68b; *Even Ha'ezer* 8:5).

Rabbi Monique Susskind Goldberg
December 2008

FOR FURTHER READING

1. Hide & Seek Foundation for Lysosomal Disease Research http://www.hideandseek.org/index.php

2. Rosner, Fred, *Modern Medicine and Jewish Ethics*, second revised and augmented edition, New York, 1991, Chapter 14.

26. Are Jews Permitted to Enter Mosques and Churches and to Attend Non-Jewish Ceremonies?

QUESTION

Dear Rabbi,

Halakhically speaking, are we permitted to enter non-Jewish places of worship for educational and ecumenical purposes? Also, being a convert, I have a lot of non-Jewish relatives, which means being invited to church weddings and funerals, as well as baptisms – am I permitted to attend these?

ANSWER

It is forbidden by Jewish Law to enter a place of idolatry. See *Tosefta Avodah Zarah* 6:3, and elsewhere. The *Shulḥan Arukh, Yoreh De'ah* 150:1 states: "It is an obligation to distance yourself from idolatry four *amot* [=two meters]". This is why, in order to decide whether one can enter a church or a mosque, it must be determined if Islam or Christianity are considered idolatry.

Most authorities do not consider Islam as idolatry and allow entering mosques. See Maimonides, *Responsa*, No. 448 (ed. Blau, p. 726) and Laws of Forbidden Foods 11:7. His opinion was generally accepted.

Many authorities consider Christianity a form of idolatry because Christians worship Jesus. In consequence, those authorities forbid Jews to enter churches. See, for example, Maimonides' commentary on *Mishnah Avodah Zarah* 1:4 and Laws of Idolatry 9:4. This is also the opinion of some contemporary authorities, such as Rabbi Eliezer Waldenberg (*Tzitz Eliezer*, vol. 14, No. 91) and Rabbi Moshe Feinstein (*Igrot Moshe, Yoreh De'ah*, vol. 3, No. 129).

But there is also an opinion that says that Christianity is **not** idolatry because Christians worship God. This is the opinion expressed in Tosafot (*Avodah Zarah* 2a *s.v. asur*). This is also the opinion of Rabbi Menahem Hameiri (Provence, 1249-1315; *Beit Habeḥirah* on *Avodah Zarah* 2a), of Rabbi Moshe Isserles in *Oraḥ Ḥayyim* 156:1 and of many other authorities, among them Israel's

Chief Rabbi Isaac Herzog (1888-1959) and Conservative Rabbi Elliot Dorff.

The *Va'ad Hahalakhah* (Law Committee) of the Rabbinical Assembly of Israel has published a responsum on this very question.

It was decided by the Committee that a Jew may enter mosques and churches for educational purposes and to learn about the other religions' traditions and customs. There was, however, no consensus between the members of the Committee on the subject of entering churches at the time of worship. They advised that one should consult with a Rabbi for each particular occasion.

I believe that in order not to cut yourself off from your family and friends, it would be permissible for you to attend the life-cycle events that you describe, but you should make sure not to participate in any religious part of the ceremony. During those parts, you could stand off to one side making it clear that you are not participating in the ceremony and in the service. Maybe you should consider telling your family before the event that you will not be participating in the service so as to avoid any misunderstanding or discomfort at the event itself.

Rabbi Monique Susskind Goldberg
October 2005

FOR FURTHER READING

1. Dorff, Elliot, "Use of Synagogues by Christian Groups", *Responsa 1980-1990*, New York, 2005, pp. 165-184.

2. Frankel, David, "Entering Mosques and Churches", in: *Responsa of the Va'ad Halakhah of the Rabbinical Assembly of Israel*, vol. 6 (5755-5758), pp. 211-230 [Hebrew with an English abstract; also available at http://www.responsafortoday.com].

3. Herzog, Isaac Halevi, *Shana Beshana*, 1986, pp. 136-140 [Hebrew].

27. Do Jews Hate Gentiles?

QUESTION

Dear Rabbi,

I hope you will answer me honestly, I am a Gentile (a Christian), and I understand if you don't want to talk with me, but can you shed some light on the Talmud for me? Are Gentiles considered sub-human? Are the Gentiles less important than Jews? Is hitting a Jewish person like hitting God? Please explain. Is it okay to lie to Gentiles, and even the best Gentile should be killed? Why, I am wondering, if the Talmud is a holy book second only to the Torah or equal with the Torah, would it be so anti-Gentile, and if this is true, then would you say that God doesn't love the Gentiles? I'm so taken aback by this information. I write to IDF soldiers, I love Israel, and I love the Jews. I always stick up for them online, and it is because of my faith, that I would defend her and fight for her. So please don't tell me what I want to hear – tell me the truth.

ANSWER

We are glad to answer your question.

There is a universal element in Judaism: God created humanity from only one man. We derive from this that destroying one life is like destroying the whole world (*Mishnah Sanhedrin* 4:5 and cf. above, p. 69). Human life is sacred, no matter what the person's identity is.

I am sure you are aware that the Bible commands the Israelites numerous times to love the stranger in their midst, since they had been strangers in the land of Egypt (see Leviticus 19:34; Deuteronomy 10:19). There are many laws in the Bible that stress the need for fair and humane treatment of strangers in our midst (e.g., Deuteronomy 24:14, paying a just wage; Exodus 22:20, not to oppress them; Exodus 20:10 and 23:12, not to have them work on the Sabbath, etc.). Furthermore, Maimonides codifies that the just people among the nations have a portion in the World to Come (Laws of Kings and Their Wars 8:11).

On the other hand, it is clear that the Talmud has many sayings against the Gentiles of its time, who were all idolaters. This was due in part to the persecutions to which the Jews were subjected and in part because they considered that the Gentiles in those times practiced immoral sexual behavior and had no consideration for human life. Therefore, the rabbis did their utmost to be as far apart from Gentile society as possible, and dedicated a whole Talmudic treatise (*Avodah Zarah*) to these kinds of issues.

In Medieval times, when the Jews lived mostly in Christian and Moslem societies, Jewish law evolved. Many Talmudic passages were interpreted as applying only to idolaters. Some rabbis excluded the Moslems and others excluded the Christians from these rulings (see above, No. 26).

For example, the Meiri (Rabbi Menaḥem ben Solomon Meiri, Provence, 1249-1315) is known for his Talmudic commentaries. In them, he explains that the Gentiles of his time (he lived in a Christian environment), who have a monotheistic belief, are **not** included in the Talmudic passages regarding idolaters (see *Beit Habeḥirah, Avodah Zarah* 20a, *Gittin* 62a). The Meiri considered Christians among the "nations bound by the ways of religion," and not idolaters.

Maimonides ruled that Muslims are not idolaters (see his *Responsa*, ed. Blau, No. 448).

Jews and Gentiles have different ways of worshipping God; yet we are all His creatures, all created in His image, and should treat each other in a humane fashion. As we mentioned above, "the just people of all nations have a portion in the World to Come"; this certainly applies to the monotheistic religions that have the same ethical values found in Judaism.

Jews around the world are now celebrating the High Holidays and are hoping for a better year. Let us hope this year will bring more understanding among all the inhabitants of this planet, so that we can all live in peace and harmony despite our differences.

For further details, see the English abstract of Rabbi Theodore Friedman's *responsum* "Is Judaism by its Nature Racist?". He explains in no uncertain terms that the strong language against idolaters was said in a specific historical context and does not reflect basic Jewish values that derive from the Bible in general and prophetic teachings in particular. Those Jews who espouse such views, even in our time, are, in our opinion following a mistaken point of view.

Sincerely,
Rabbi Diana Villa
September 2003

FOR FURTHER READING

Friedman, Theodore, "Is Judaism by its Nature Racist?", in *The Responsa of the Va'ad Halakhah of the Rabbinical Assembly of Israel*, Vol. 2 (5747), pp. 37-46 [Hebrew with an English abstract; also available at hhtp://www.responsafortoday.com].

28. How Can I Get the Approval of My Jewish Girlfriend's Family?

QUESTION

Dear Rabbi,

I am a non-Jewish man (24 years old) who has fallen in love with a Jewish girl. Her family does not support us being in a relationship together; they have gone as far as to say they will disown her if she continues to see me. We seem to be perfect for one another, we have known each other for a number of years now and have been good friends up until recently when our feelings boiled over and we made the move to be together. Her family is extremely religious but she is not so. She does not eat kosher and on occasion will break Shabbat. Her family knows about these things, but does nothing about it. How can her family have such a strong opinion regarding her relationships, yet turn a blind eye to the rest of her outwardly non-Jewish behavior?

I am not a particularly religious person; I don't go to church yet I still believe in God and I am more than willing to learn about any faith. Is there any way in which we could possibly be together without her having to give up her family/friends/religious beliefs?

Any advice would be extremely welcome!

ANSWER

I understand your distress and do not have a simple solution to your problem.

Jewish Law forbids mixed marriages (see Maimonides, Laws of Forbidden Sexual Relations 12:1; *Even Ha'ezer* 16:1).

Judaism is also against mixed marriage from an ideological point of view.

You have to understand that for Jewish parents, the fact that their daughter would consider marriage outside of the Jewish people is much more difficult than the fact that for the moment she is less observant of the religious commandments. She can

90

always become more observant at a later point in life, but marrying a non-Jew has implications for her children and for future generations. It is a matter of survival and your friend's parents want their grandchildren to be Jewish (which they would be because their mother is Jewish) and educated as Jews.

The only real solution that would likely satisfy your friend's family would be for you to convert. This is a very big step, and you have to think very carefully if you are willing to do this (if you believe in Jesus, you cannot do it). It involves months of study, acceptance of the Jewish commandments and circumcision.

I believe you and your girlfriend must have a serious talk about your future relationship. Is she willing to break with her family? Are you willing to convert and if not, are you willing to provide your future children with a Jewish education?

As you can see, there are no easy solutions. Write me again if you have other questions.

Rabbi Monique Susskind Goldberg
November 2007

FOR FURTHER READING

1. Kornbluth, Doron, *Why Marry Jewish?*, Southfield, Michigan, 2003.

2. Shemtov, Eliezer, *Dear Rabbi, Why Can't I Marry Her?*, Southfield, Michigan, 2008.

3. Silverstein, Alan, *It All Begins With a Date: Jewish Concerns About Intermarriage*, West Orange, New Jersey, 1994.

29. Are Interfaith Services Permitted?

QUESTION

I am hoping you will be able to assist me. I am trying to find out information about prohibitions against interfaith prayer as well as any sources citing the permissibility of interfaith prayer. If you have any information you can offer, I greatly appreciate the help.

ANSWER

When Rabbi Haskel Lookstein, a well-known Orthodox rabbi, agreed to participate in the interfaith service in honor of Barak Obama's inauguration as President of the United States, which took place in the National Cathedral, he was very strongly criticized by members of the Orthodox Rabbinical Council of America. They objected to him participating in an event together with Muslims, Christians and representatives of other religions.

Rabbi Lookstein answered the critics with Rabbi Joseph Karo's ruling:

> One does not go in the ways of idolaters, one does not imitate them... one does not wear their garments... However, whoever is close to the government and must dress like them to resemble them, may do so (*Yoreh De'ah* 178:1-2).

He explained that, according to this passage in the *Shulḥan Arukh*, in normal circumstances one is not allowed to imitate the behavior of idolaters – "wearing garments worn by idolaters" in the language of the *Shulḥan Arukh*. However, there is, according to the same source, an exception in the case of a person who by his/her position needs to be close to the government – he/she is then allowed to imitate the behavior of idolaters. Rabbi Lookstein writes:

> The *Shulḥan Arukh* is dealing here with a specific Torah prohibition regarding the wearing of garments worn by idolaters and yet that prohibition is overridden in order to

effectively represent the Jewish community before government officials.

It is clear from this statement that for Rabbi Lookstein, participating in this ceremony was a political act. In his eyes, the non-Jews representing other faiths in that interfaith prayer service were idolaters and he, for the sake of representing the Jewish people, "imitated" their behavior.

With all due respect to Rabbi Lookstein, I would like to point out the following:

1. Most authorities do not consider Islam idolatry and allow entering mosques (see No. 26 above).

2. Although many authorities consider Christianity a form of idolatry because Christians worship Jesus, there is also an opinion that says that Christianity is not idolatry because Christians worship the one God (*ibid.*)

   We are of the opinion that neither Muslims nor Christians are idolaters.

3. In our time, it is very rare to find people who actually worship idols.

This is why we do not consider the non-Jews who participate in interfaith prayers to be idolaters and we do not accept that for a Jew to participate in them is comparable to "wearing garments worn by idolaters".

Besides this, the goal of the kind of interfaith prayer you are referring to in your question is not political but rather is for the sake of having a shared spiritual experience between people of different religions, in order to promote peace and understanding between people.

It is thus, in our opinion, not forbidden for a Jew to participate in an interfaith event, even if it is not "to represent the Jewish community before government officials". However, we do believe that some conditions should apply for a Jew to be able to participate.

a) The prayers and the text used in such a ceremony should be neutral and accepted by all participants, e.g., selections from the Book of Psalms.

b) As there is no consensus about Jews entering a church, the place where the interfaith prayer service is held should also be neutral.

Rabbi Monique Susskind Goldberg
February 2009

FOR FURTHER READING

1. "Are Jews Permitted to Enter Mosques and Churches and to Attend Non-Jewish Sevices?", above, No. 26.

2. Frankel, David, "Entering Mosques and Churches" in *Responsa of the Va'ad Halakhah of the Rabbinical Assembly of Israel*, vol. 6 (5755-5758), pp. 211-230 [Hebrew with an English abstract; also available at: http://www.responsafortoday.com].

3. Lookstein, Haskel, http://lookstein.org/lookjed/read.php?1,17573,17632.

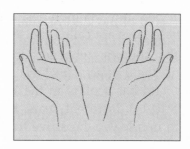

30. Should We Teach the Seven Noahide Laws to Non-Jews?

QUESTION

Dear Rabbi,

Someone asked me the following questions concerning *Bnei Noah*, the Sons of Noah: Is it a *mitzvah* to teach non-Jews the seven Noahide Laws? What status does a person that is taught these laws and tries to observe them achieve? Does a Gentile Noahide believer have to deny believing in Jesus as his/her Lord?

I was a bit disturbed by these questions, thinking to myself that we have enough educating to do here in Germany within the Jewish community, without reaching out to the larger community. But I became interested in the question on a theoretical level.

ANSWER

We do not find in Jewish sources a commandment to teach the *mitzvot* to non-Jews. According to the Sages, all humanity, descendants of Noah, are commanded by God to keep seven Laws. These Laws are the prohibition of idolatry, murder, theft, sexual promiscuity, blasphemy, eating flesh taken from an animal while it is still alive and the requirement to have just laws (see *Sanhedrin* 56a and Maimonides, Laws of Kings and Their Wars 9:1). These laws are called the seven Noahide Laws.

According to the sources, whoever observes these seven Noahide laws joins the *Hasidei Umot Ha'olam*, the righteous among the nations, and has a place in the World to Come (see Maimonides, *ibid.* 8:10-11). In recent years, the term "Noahide" has come to refer to non-Jews who strive to live in accord with the seven Noahide Laws.

But even those who observe the above-mentioned seven laws are still not Jewish. Whoever aspires to become part of the Jewish people and to live a fully Jewish life, must convert.

Many Jewish authorities do not consider Christianity to be idolatrous because they still have a monotheistic belief.[2] Therefore, a Christian does not have to deny Jesus as his/her Lord to be considered as a Noahide as long as he observes the seven Noahide Laws.

Sincerely,
Rabbi Diana Villa
March 2002

FOR FURTHER READING

1. *Encycylopaedia Judaica*, second edition, Jerusalem, 2007, "Noachide Laws", Vol. 15, pp. 284-287.

2. Frankel, David, "Entering Mosques and Churches" in *Responsa of the Va'ad Halakhah of the Rabbinical Assembly of Israel*, vol. 6 (5755-5758), pp. 211-230 [Hebrew with an English abstract; also available at: http://www.responsafor today.com].

3. Novak, David, *The Image of the Non-Jew in Judaism: A Historical and Constructive Study of the Noahide Laws*, New York, 1983.

---

2 See Rabbeinu Tam's ruling in *Tosafot Bekhorot* 2a, *s.v. shema* and the Meiri's ruling in *Beit HaBeḥirah* to *Gittin* 62a, *s.v. ovdei hagilulim*.

JEWISH SYMBOLS AND TRADITIONS

31. Are We Required to Kiss the *Mezuzah*?

QUESTION

Dear Rabbi,

We have *mezuzot* hanging on three of the doors in our house, including one that welcomes clients to our home business.

I am proud of these symbols of my Judaism, but I feel awkward reaching to kiss it each time I exit or enter the house. Please tell me to what extent this gesture is required.

ANSWER

The first evidence of the custom of placing one's hand on the *mezuzah* is in the Talmud, *Avodah Zarah* 11a. This was probably the source for the custom described by Rabbi Jacob Moellin, the Maharil, that a hand should be placed on the *mezuzah* before leaving town (see *Minhagei Maharil*, ed. Shpitzer, Jerusalem, 1989, p. 634, *Likutim*, parag. 91). He adds that one should do this every time one leaves one's house. The Rema quotes the latter opinion and concurs (*Yoreh De'ah* 285:2). Rabbi Isaac Luria, known as the *Ari Hakadosh*, recommended kissing the *mezuzah* when leaving the house (quoted in *Birkei Yosef* on *Yoreh De'ah* 285:4).

While having a *mezuzah* on your doorpost is a requirement, kissing the doorpost *mezuzah* is not. Therefore, you can refrain from kissing it, or reserve that gesture for when you are leaving town, as the original custom seemed to be, while saying "The Lord is my keeper, the Lord is my shade upon my right hand" (see Maharil; the sentence is based on Psalm 121:5).

Sincerely,
Rabbi Diana Villa
June, 2004

FOR FURTHER READING

Roth, Simcha, "On Kissing the Mezuzah in Public Places", *Kehilaton* (of the Masorti Movement), Rosh Hashanah 5768, p. 6 [Hebrew].

32. May I Shave with a Razor?

QUESTION

Dear Rabbi,

I know that according to the *Shulḥan Arukh* beards appear to be for the most part mandatory. Most Orthodox rabbis accept this as binding, although they permit the use of scissors and an electric razor. This is problematic for me, since growing a beard or shaving with an electric razor causes my face to break out in a rash.

Your input regarding the use of a regular razor would be much appreciated.

ANSWER

You are correct that Jewish law forbids the use of a razor blade (or a shaving knife in old times) directly upon the skin (see Maimonides, Laws of Mourning 6:13; *Yoreh De'ah*, 181:10). A scissors that leaves at least a minimal amount of hair is allowed since it is considered shaving that does not "destroy".[3] According to many modern decisors, an electric shaver, in which the razor does not come directly in contact with the skin, is also allowed (it too is considered "shaving that does not destroy"), especially in cases where there are medical reasons to be lenient in this matter. Even then, one has to be careful not to use those electric shavers that have very sharp blades and cut the hair that is directly on the skin.

A hair that cannot be cut by a scissors is not considered a hair (see Maimonides, Laws of the Red Heifer 1:4 and Laws of the Uncleanness of Leprosy 2:1). In a case such as yours, in which shaving produces great discomfort, some authorities allow for an exceptional solution: cutting the hair with a scissors until so little hair is left that what is later removed with a razor can no longer be considered destroying a beard (based on the principle in

---

3 According to Leviticus 19:27: "You shall not round off the side-locks on your head, or **destroy** the side-growth of your beard" – only shaving that destroys the beard is forbidden.

Makkot 21a that this is shaving that does not destroy the beard, which is what the Torah forbids in Leviticus 19:27). R. David Zvi Hoffmann explains in his responsa, *Melamed Le-Ho'il, Yoreh De'ah* No. 64 that, even though he would not rule this way unless he got the support of his teacher, Rabbi Israel Hildesheimer, there are two reasons for leniency:

1. there is a medical reason involved;
2. the razor removes hair that is so short that cutting it does not transgress the prohibition.

He recommends having a non-Jew do this, so that a Jew does not actively take part in the process.

I hope this will help you in deciding what to do about your beard in the future.

Sincerely,
Rabbi Diana Villa
July 2003

FOR FURTHER READING

1. *Entziklopedia Talmudit*, vol. 11, Jerusalem, 1965, "*Hashhatat Zakan*", columns 125-128 [Hebrew].

2. Rappaport, Shabtai Hakohen, "Shaving Beards with an Electric Shaver", *Tehumim* 13 (1992-1993), pp. 200-208 [Hebrew].

3. "Is There an Obligation to Grow a Beard?", below, No. 37.

33. How Do I Make a *Tallit* by Myself?

QUESTION

Dear Rabbi,

I have a few questions regarding the *tallit*. I am a crocheter and I have a Conservative Jewish friend for whom I would like to make a *tallit*. I did a great deal of research on it, and I think I am ready, but I'd like to get some clarification.

First, does it have to be of natural materials? Some websites say yes, but then I find sites that sell acrylic and rayon *tallitot* to synagogues.

Second, size seems to vary. I was planning on making this one 30x80 inches. Is this too narrow?

Third, can anyone tie the *tzitzit*? I was going to tie them, but I am not Jewish. I don't want to taint the garment by tying it if that doesn't count.

Fourth, does the blue strand in the *tzitzit* have to be dyed with *tekhelet*, or can it just be blue? Should I omit blue all together if I don't have access to *tekhelet*?

Speaking of color, I was planning a cream body, blue and black stripes, a white *atara* and *kanaf*, white threads and one blue *tzitzit* thread, and a cream fringe. I've read that this should be acceptable, but I want to make sure.

Finally, does my completed *tallit* need rabbinical certification, or can he simply wear it?

Thank you so much for all of your help!

ANSWER

Thank you for your questions about the *tallit*. It is a beautiful idea to make a *tallit* for your friend. Here are the answers to your questions.

1. Material

The *tallit*:

Orah Hayyim 9:1-2 states that the Biblical commandment of *tzitzit* pertains only to four-cornered garments made of wool or of linen (this is based on a midrash on Deuteronomy 22:11-12); if one uses other material it is only a Rabbinic enactment. There is, however, an opinion (in the Rema) that the Biblical obligation pertains to all materials. But the material must be made from woven threads; this is why one cannot fulfill the *mitzvah* of *tzitzit* with a leather garment (see *Menaḥot* 40b). Modern authorities are divided on the question whether clothing from synthetic material requires *tzitzit* or not. In his *responsum* on this subject, Rabbi Moshe Feinstein compares synthetic materials to leather and states that they do not require *tzitzit* (see *Igrot Moshe, Oraḥ Ḥayyim*, part 2, No. 1). However, Rabbi Eliezer Waldenberg ruled that as long as the material is made from woven thread it should be consider as clothing and thus the Biblical requirement to put "fringes in the corners of their garments" (Numbers 15:38) applies. (*Responsa Tzitz Eliezer*, vol. 12, No. 3). I tend to agree with the decision of Rabbi Waldenberg that a four-cornered garment made from any woven material requires *tzitzit*. Traditionally, wool is preferred for a *tallit*.

The *tzitzit*:

According to *Oraḥ Ḥayyim* 9:2-3, woolen and linen *tzitzit* can be put on garments made from any material. However, because of the law forbidding mingling wool and linen (Deuteronomy 22:11), no woolen *tzitzit* may be put on a linen *tallit* and no linen *tzitzit* on a woolen *tallit*. *Tzitzit* from other material can be put only on a garment of the same material (i.e. silk on silk, cotton on cotton). According to the Rema, it is better not to use linen *tzitzit* and to use only wool *tzitzit* (*Oraḥ Ḥayyim, ibid.*). As to the color of the *tzitzit*, the *Shulḥan Arukh* (*Oraḥ Ḥayyim* 9:5) gives the Sephardic tradition to make the *tzitzit* the same color as the *tallit*. Ashkenazim, however, use only white *tzitzit* (Rema). Again, the preferred tradition is to use wool. In Numbers 15:38, mentioned above, we have the commandment to put "a thread of blue" in the fringes. The blue thread is supposed to be colored with the *tekhelet* (blue) dye. This tradition disappeared about 1,000 years ago. In the 19th century, R. Gershon Hanokh Leiner began to use the cuttlefish to make *tekhelet*. Today, many use *tekhelet* made from murex snails, following the opinion of Rabbi

Yitzḥak Herzog from 1919 (see For Further Reading). If you cannot purchase *tekhelet tzitzit*, you should buy simple white ones.

2. Size

The sources state that in order to be considered a garment needing *tzitzit*, the *tallit* must be at least large enough for "a nine-year-old child to cover his head and part of his body" with it (*Oraḥ Ḥayyim* 16:1). There is a discussion among the authorities about the meaning of this measure, but they arrived at the conclusion that it is more or less 1.5 *ama* (+/-75cm) in length by 1 *ama* in width (+/-50cm) (see for instance *Yalkut Yosef, She'erit Yosef*, part 1, p. 244). It seems that the measure you propose is somewhat too small, especially for the width. The purpose of the *tzitzit* is to remind us of the commandments. This is the reason why, according to the *Shulḥan Arukh*, the *tallit* should be big enough so one can put two *tzitzit* in the back and two *tzitzit* in front – in order to be "surrounded by the commandments" (*Oraḥ Ḥayyim* 8:4).

3. Now, I am sorry to disappoint you, but if a non-Jew ties the *tzitzit*, the *tallit* is not kosher (*Oraḥ Ḥayyim* 14:1, and *Mishnah Berurah, ad. loc.*), the reason given is that the commandment of *tzitzit* was given to the Jews and not to the non-Jews (Numbers 15:38).

4. The *tzitzit* cannot be just any threads you hang on the *tallit*. They have to be specially spun for this specific use (*Oraḥ Ḥayyim* 11:1), meaning they have to be bought in a store that sells Jewish religious items. And unless you know a Jewish person who knows how to tie the knots (they have to be tied in a very specific way – see *Oraḥ Ḥayyim* 11:12-15), it would probably be best for you to ask a salesperson in the store to recommend somebody who can put the *tzitzit* on your *tallit*.

5. Any color you choose is fine. I'm sure it will come out beautifully.

6. When your friend wears the *tallit* for the first time, he has to recite the *Sheheḥeyanu* blessing in addition to the blessing for putting on a *tallit*. You can show it to a Rabbi if you feel like it, but there is no need for rabbinical certification.

Good luck in creating your *tallit*.

Rabbi Monique Susskind Goldberg
February 2003

FOR FURTHER READING

1. *Encyclopaedia Judaica*, second edition, Jerusalem, 2007, "Tekhelet", Vol. 19, pp. 586-587.

2. Herzog, Isaac, *Judaism: Law and Ethics*, London, Jerusalem, New York, 1974, pp. 1-11.

3. Herzog, Isaac, *The Royal Purple and the Biblical Blue*, edited by Ehud Spanier, Jerusalem, 1987.

4. *"Ptil Tekhelet"*, http://www.tekhelet.com

34. How Often Should One Check a *Mezuzah*?

QUESTION

Dear Rabbi,

I am a little confused. My rabbi spoke about the *mezuzah* several weeks ago, and he said that it is not necessary to check the *mezuzah* to ensure that it is kosher. I have a copy of the English translation of Maimonides, and he writes that one must check it once in seven years. Does this mean that the Conservative Movement doesn't believe in having a kosher *mezuzah*? I'm confused.

ANSWER

The *mezuzah* is written on *klaf* (parchment) which may have been stolen or decayed (due to rain, insects or the house being repaired or painted). Furthemore, the parchment may tear or a letter may have been erased (see Rashi on *Yoma* 11a, *s.v. nivdeket* and Maimonides, Laws of *Tefillin, Mezuzah* and the Torah Scroll 5:9).

To ensure that none of this has occurred, a *mezuzah* in the home must be checked twice in seven years, However, a *mezuzah* in a public place, must be checked only once in 50 years (see Maimonides *ibid.* and *Yoreh De'ah* 291:1). The authorities fear that since a public *mezuzah* is a shared responsibility, if it needs to be checked as often as a privately owned *mezuzah*, everyone will rely on someone else to do it and therefore it may not be done (see Rashi, *loc. cit., s.v. pa'amayim beyovel*).

Regarding Jewish law and practice this is a very clear-cut issue. You may have misunderstood your rabbi. I hope this eases your confusion.

Sincerely,
Rabbi Diana Villa
October 2003

35. Is It Mandatory to Wear a *Tallit Katan*?

QUESTION

Dear Rabbi,

What is the position of the Conservative Movement regarding the wearing of a *tallit katan*? It appears mandatory amongst Orthodox men. Although one could argue that since we do not wear four-cornered garments anymore, the *mitzvah* may not be relevant anymore, but we still insist on wearing the *tallit gadol*. If I am paraphrasing correctly (from memory), doesn't the Torah say that *tzitzit* is a commandment "for all generations... and so that our eyes may see them"? Couldn't it be argued that the *tallit katan* has a religious/spiritual function on its own that developed throughout the ages, like in the Talmudic story of the man whose *tzitzit* slapped him in the face when he wanted to sin with a prostitute?

Or is it an unnecessary "stringency"? I am curious to hear your opinion.

ANSWER

You correctly understand that the commandment to wear *tzitzit* (Numbers 15:38-39; Deuteronomy 22:12) applies only to four-cornered garments and is not mandatory if you do not wear such a garment. In Biblical times, most clothing had four corners, and even later on men wore large cloaks where *tzitzit* could be tied. However, when the fashion changed and men no longer wore this kind of clothing, in order to keep the Biblical commandment to have fringes: "...that you may look upon it, and remember all the commandments of the Lord, and do them" (Numbers 15:39) the custom was established to wear the *tzitzit* on a *tallit* (prayer shawl) at prayer time.

The *Shulḥan Arukh* adds that even though there is no obligation to wear *tzitzit* if one does not wear a four-cornered garment, "it is good and right for each person to wear a *tallit katan* all day in order to have a constant reminder to observe all the commandments" (*Oraḥ Ḥayyim* 24:1). It appears that the *tallit katan* is first mentioned in Provence in the 12th century (*Sefer*

Ha'ittur, fols. 73a and 75b) and the earliest picture of this garment is from Ashkenaz, ca. 1460 (*The Ashkenazi Haggadah*, New York, 1985, fol. 8b). Eventually, this became a well-established custom. The *tallit katan* is, in general, worn under the clothing, with the *tzitzit* often showing outside.

The religious/spiritual purpose is not so much in the *tallit* but in the *tzitzit*. This purpose, as we have seen, already exists in the Bible (Numbers 15:39): to remind us of the commandments. This is also the moral behind the famous story you mentioned. When the *tzitzit* slapped him in the face, the Ḥassid was reminded of the law and this prevented him from sinning (*Menaḥot* 44a).

Thus, the *tallit katan* is a beautiful medieval custom and we encourage you to adopt it.

Rabbi Monique Susskind Goldberg
June 2005

36. Is Selling a Torah Scroll Allowed?

QUESTION

Dear Rabbi,

Your assistance is appreciated. My Conservative synagogue has seventeen Torah Scrolls! Over our history, our inventory has grown. We recently had a project to have a *Sofer* correct our Torahs, so now we have many more than we need to conduct services throughout the year. We now would like to reduce our Torah Scroll collection for the benefit of others and ourselves. Is it OK to sell a Torah to another congregation? I see them for sale in advertisements.

ANSWER

We read in the *Shulḥan Arukh* (*Yoreh De'ah* 270:1):

> It is forbidden to sell a Torah Scroll even if one possesses many others, even to sell an old Scroll for the sake of buying a new one. One is allowed to sell a Torah Scroll only in order to learn Torah or to get married, if one does not have anything else to sell.

The Rema adds: "also in order to free prisoners". The interdiction on selling a Torah Scroll appears in *Mishnah Megillah* 3:1 (*Megillah* 27a). In his commentary on this *Mishnah*, Maimonides explains that this law stems from the principle of *"ma'alin bakodesh v'lo moridin"* – "one lifts up in holiness and does not diminish it"(see *Mishnah Shekalim* 6:4 and elsewhere). No object is holier than a Torah Scroll.

Oraḥ Ḥayyim 153:6 (see also *Mishnah Berurah ad loc.*, subparag. 24) explains that one can sell a Torah Scroll to provide for students (to study Torah) and to provide for the wedding of orphans (see also Maimonides, Laws of *Tefillin*, *Mezuzah* and the Torah Scroll 10:2).

Accordingly, the authorities do not generally allow the selling of a Torah even if the reason is to buy a new one.

As for the Torah Scrolls you saw for sale in advertisements, here is the explanation I received from one of the companies selling Torahs Scrolls online:

> With a new Torah Scroll, one purchases it before it is complete and then after it was purchased, the scribe finishes the last few letters. Since the Torah Scroll wasn't yet kosher when it was purchased, it didn't have the status of a Torah Scroll and could be sold. With a used Torah Scroll, there are generally some repairs that need to be done to make it kosher, so the principle is the same: it is sold before it becomes kosher again. The prohibition against selling Torah Scrolls applies to a kosher Torah Scroll only.

In conclusion, if your synagogue has no financial problems and can provide for people to study Torah and can also provide, in case of need, a young couple with financial help to get married without selling these Torah Scrolls, it is better to loan them to other synagogues in need.

Rabbi Monique Susskind Goldberg
November 2006

FOR FURTHER READING

Felder, Gedalia, *Yesodei Yeshurun*, part 2, New York, 1956, pp. 149-151 [Hebrew].

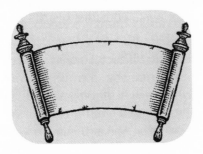

37. Is There an Obligation to Grow a Beard?

QUESTION

Dear Rabbi,

The Torah mentions growing beards in relation to mourning and the Nazirite laws. Is there an obligation to grow a beard according to Jewish law? Is it limited to mourning?

ANSWER

There is no commandment to grow a beard, only a prohibition to destroy it. The Torah teaches "You shall not round off the side-locks on your head, or destroy the side-growth of your beard" (Leviticus 19:27). The *Mishnah* explains that whoever does so is flogged (*Mishnah Makkot* 3:5 = *Makkot* 20a). The codes rule that Jewish men are not allowed to shave with a razor or shaving knife (*Yoreh De'ah* 181:10 and above, No. 32).

The Torah commanded priests who are in mourning not to shave their heads (Leviticus 10:6). The codes rule on this basis that no men in mourning may shave at all (Maimonides, Laws of Mourning 5:2).

Men who have lost a close relative (father, mother, sister, brother, spouse, son or daughter) are not supposed to shave for thirty days, as a sign of mourning (*Yoreh De'ah* 390:1). This is independent of the prohibition of applying a knife or razor to the skin.

According to the codes, a prayer leader is supposed to have a beard (*Orah Hayyim* 53:6, 8), which is why in the *Hineni* prayer in the High Holiday *Musaf* services, the ideal *shliah tzibbur* is described as one who has a beard. Even though having a beard is not an obligation, kabbalists consider beards to have a spiritual meaning.

Sincerely,
Rabbi Diana Villa
August 2003

FOR FURTHER READING

1. *Entziklopedia Talmudit* , vol. 11, Jerusalem, 1965, *Hashḥatat Zakan*, columns 125-128 [Hebrew].

2. Halberstam, Yekutiel Yehudah, *Responsa Divrei Yatziv, Likutim Vehashmatot*, No. 91 [Hebrew].

3. Horowitz, Elliott, "The Early Eighteenth Century Confronts the Beard" etc., *Jewish History* 8/1-2 (1994), pp. 95-115.

4. Horowitz, Elimelekh, "On the Meanings of the Beard in Jewish Communities", *Pe'amim* 59 (Spring 5754), pp. 124-148 [Hebrew].

38. What Do the Words Written on the Back of the *Mezuzah* Mean?

QUESTION

Dear Rabbi,

Why are there three words written in code on the parchment of the *mezuzah*? What do they mean?

ANSWER

According to Joshua Trachtenberg (p. 146), the *mezuzah* "descended from a primitive charm, affixed to the door-post to keep demons out of the house". The Rabbinic authorities, wanting to give religious content to this popular custom, gave it the form of a strip of parchment inscribed with the Biblical verses Deut. 6:4-9, 11:13-20, as a reminder of the principle of monotheism. But the belief in the protective power of the *mezuzah* did not disappear. Two passages in Talmudic literature attest to this: Jerusalem Talmud, *Pe'ah* 1:1, fol. 15d and Babylonian Talmud, *Avodah Zarah* 11a. In the latter passage, Onkelos the proselyte explains the meaning of the *mezuzah* to the Roman Emperor's soldiers: "a flesh and blood king sits inside his palace, and his slaves guard him from outside; but in the case of God, the King of Kings, his slaves sit inside and He guards them from outside".

Although, originally, the *mezuzah* was to contain only the prescribed text, in time, especially in certain mystic circles, it was gradually transformed into an amulet. In the Geonic period, the inside of the *mezuzah* was not touched, but new features began to appear on the back. First appeared the inscription *Shaddai*, one of God's names, who was suppose to drive off demons. By the method of *notarikon*, it was read *Shomer Daltot Yisrael* "guardian of the doors of Israel". This practice was adopted throughout the Jewish world. Subsequently, another inscription was added on the back of the *mezuzah*: כוזו במוכסז כוזו, *Kuzu Bemukhsaz Kuzu*, the words you are speaking about. It is a cryptogram whose meaning is easy to figure out if you know the key to the code: you have to go one letter backward in the Hebrew alphabet. The *caf* is a *yud*, the *hey* is a *vav* and so on. So instead of "*Kuzu*

114

Bemukhsaz Kuzu," you have *"Adonai Elohenu Adonai"*, corresponding to the words of the *Shema* inscribed on the face of the *mezuzah*. In mystical circles, this name was also considered one of God's powerful names. This inscription did not appear on every *mezuzah*. Trachtenberg (pp. 148-149) believes there were two distinct traditions: one which prescribed the addition of the name *Shaddai* alone, in Southern Europe and Spain, and the second in the North where both names appear. "In time the northern practice invaded the South as well".

The next step in transforming the *mezuzah* into an amulet occurred in the Middle Ages in some Jewish mystical circles, mainly among the early Ashkenazic Ḥassidim. The *mezuzot* from those circles include additions like names of angels, different names of God or drawings of the *Magen David* and other kabbalistic signs. In some of the *mezuzot* from the 12th century, the additions were put not only on the back of the parchment, but also on the front near the Biblical verses (see some examples in Trachtenberg, pp. 150-151).

These customs were vigorously opposed by Maimonides, according to whom the *mezuzah*'s only purpose was to emphasize the love of and belief in God (see Laws of *Tefillin, Mezuzah* and the Torah Scroll 5:4). He did, however, accept the *Shaddai* inscription on the back of the *mezuzah*. Most Rabbinical authorities followed Maimonides' condemnation, and by the 15th century, this attitude prevailed even in Kabbalistic circles, and the *mezuzah*, like the one we have today, contained only the two Biblical passages (Deut. 6:4-9 and 11:13-21) and the two names on the back (*Shaddai* and *Kuzu Bemukhsaz Kuzu*).

Rabbi Monique Susskind Goldberg
January 2002

FOR FURTHER READING

1. Feierstein, Morris M., "Safed Kabbalah and the Sephardi Heritage" in: *Sephardic and Mizraḥi Jewry from the Golden Age*

of Spain to Modern Times, edited by Zion Zohar, New York, 2005, p. 207.

2. Sperber, Daniel, *Minhagei Yisrael*, vol. 2, Jerusalem, 1991, pp. 103-106 and vol. 8, Jerusalem, 2007, pp. 91-124 [Hebrew].

3. Trachtenberg, Joshua, *Jewish Magic and Superstition*, New York, 1939, pp. 145-152.

39. What Is the Significance of Wearing a *Kippah*? Is It a Requirement?

QUESTION

Dear Rabbi,

Once a Rabbi told me that we wear a *kippah* because God is above us, but God is within us, so why do we need to wear a *kippah*?

ANSWER

This explanation that one wears a *kippah* as a reminder that God is above us probably has its origin in what is related in the Talmud (*Kiddushin* 31a):

> Rav Huna the son of Rav Yehoshua did not walk four *amot* [approximately two meters] with his head uncovered. He said: the *Shekhinah* [the divine presence] is above my head (also see *Shabbat* 156b).

However, this was not presented in the Talmud as mandatory behavior, but as the behavior of a very pious man. If we examine the sources about the obligation for Jewish men to wear a head covering, this is what we find.

1. The custom of men covering their heads varied greatly according to the time and the place.

a. In the period of the *Mishnah* and the Talmud, wearing a head covering was a custom of piety only observed by some of the Sages in Babylon, particularly after marriage (see for instance *Kiddushin* 8a, 29b and 31a).

b. After the Talmudic period, authorities differed greatly in their decisions about wearing a head covering and were influenced by local customs and by the conditions of their time. For instance, for Maimonides, living in the 12th century in North Africa, covering the head was only a custom of modesty of the Sages (Laws of Ethical Ideas 5:6, 8). Maimonides' contemporary, R. Avraham ben Natan HaYarḥi, who was probably influenced by the customs in Provence and Spain where he lived, considered it mandatory for a Jewish man to wear a head covering (*Sefer Hamanhig*, ed. Rafael, p. 87). But according to his own testimony, in France it was the custom for men to wear a headcovering only to recite blessings (*ibid.*, p. 221). Important authorities such as the Maharam of Rothenburg (Germany, 13th century) or the Gaon of Vilna (Poland, 18th century) recognized that covering the head was not an obligation but an act of piety. Nevertheless, the custom of men covering their head became the norm in Ashkenaz from the 15th century on. Walking bareheaded was considered contrary to the Jewish religion (see for example the *Responsa of R. Yisrael Bruna*, No. 34).

c. In our day, wearing a *kippah* is primarily a symbol of Jewish identity. According to some contemporary authorities, the *kippah* is not only an act of piety, but a public declaration of being a religious Jew (see R. Ovadiah Yosef, *Yehaveh Da'at*, part 4, No. 1).

2. The requirement for men to cover their heads when praying or reciting God's name.

a. There is no testimony that in the period of the *Mishnah* men were obliged to wear a headcovering at prayer time.

b. The obligation to cover the head during prayer began in Babylon (*Berakhot* 51a) and in the Geonic period it was restricted to the prayer leader, to the reader of the Torah and to the *Kohanim* blessing the community (see *Massekhet Sofrim* 14:12). It seems that this custom was particular to Babylon, while in Israel men were still praying bareheaded.

Later on, many authorities did not consider covering the head during prayer as a halakhic obligation, but recommended it during the *Amidah* prayer (Maimonides, Laws of Prayer and of the Priestly Blessing 5:5; *Orah Hayyim* 91:3, 5; the Vilna Gaon's commentary on *Orah Hayyim* 8:2).

c. In modern times, there is no doubt that the custom of covering one's head, in particular at prayer time, became deeply rooted in the consciousness of the Jewish people as an expression of piety and respect and became a binding custom.

Rabbi Monique Susskind Goldberg
September 2006

FOR FURTHER READING

1. Frankel, David, "The Wearing of a *Kippah* by Men and Women", in *Responsa of the Va'ad Halakhah of the Rabbinical Assembly of Israel*, vol. 6, (5755-5758), pp. 39-57 [Hebrew with an English abstract; also available at http://www.responsafortoday.com].

2. Klein, Isaac, *A Guide to Jewish Religious Practice*, New York, 1992, pp. 51-52.

3. Krauss, Samuel, "The Jewish Rite of Covering the Head", *HUCA* 19 (1945-1946), pp. 121-168.

4. Lauterbach, J.Z., "Worshipping with Covered Heads" in: Walter Jacob, ed., *American Reform Responsa*, New York, 1983, pp. 8-21.

5. Zimmer, Eric, "Men's Headcovering" etc., in: Jacob J. Schacter, ed., *Reverence, Righteousness and Rahamanut: Essays in Memory of Rabbi Dr. Leo Jung*, Northvale, New Jersey, 1992, pp. 325-352.

KASHRUT

40. Are All Cheeses Kosher?

QUESTION

Dear Rabbi,

The cheese issue gets me every time! I am really confused over this. For my own home, I buy *hechshered* cheeses [cheeses with rabbinical supervision] only, but I am aware of the Conservative ruling that rennet is a *"davar ḥadash"* (a new product where the old ingredients are no longer recognizable) and thus, non-*hechshered* cheeses are permitted.

Now: is this only for hard cheeses or does this leniency also apply to soft, French cheeses such as Brie, Camembert, etc.?

ANSWER

Rennet is a natural complex of enzymes produced in a mammal's stomach in order to digest mother's milk. It is used as a curdling agent in the production of cheeses. It is usually extracted from the walls of a calf's stomach. There is also rennet made from plants and artificial rennet (see Wikipedia).

Obviously, there is no problem with artificial rennet nor with the rennet made from plants. There is also no problem with rennet that comes from a calf that has been slaughtered in a kosher manner (see Maimonides, Laws of Forbidden Foods 9:16).

The problem is with rennet taken from the wall of the stomach of a calf that was not validly slaughtered. Even if a very small amount is used, it is still not acceptable, according to the principle that when the curdling agent is forbidden, it is not neutralized even by a thousand times its bulk (*Yoreh De'ah* 87:11).

The prohibition of consuming cheeses made by non-Jews is mentioned in the *Mishnah* (*Avodah Zarah* 2:4-5). The reason given: "because they curdle it with the rennet of a carcass". In other words, the non-Jews use the stomach of an animal that was not validly slaughtered as their curdling agent (see also *Avodah Zarah* 29b and *Ḥullin* 116a-b).

On this basis, most authorities forbid all cheeses made by non-Jews because it is likely that the milk was curdled with the skin of the stomach of a calf that was not validly slaughtered (see for instance Maimonides, *ibid.* 3:13, 14; *Yoreh De'ah* 115:2).

However, nowadays, the rennet used by cheeses factories, is industrially produced (see Klein for details), the pieces of skin from the calf's stomach go through chemical changes which transform them into a *davar ḥadash* [a new entity]. The chemical process involved in making the rennet changes the nature of the ingredients so much, that they are no longer recognizable, and thus should not be considered as unkosher (see *Responsa Aḥiezer*).

This is why some modern authorities are more lenient on consuming cheeses made by non-Jews (see R. Yehudah Leib Graubart and R. Isaac Klein).

Rabbi Isaac Klein in his *Responsa and Halakhic Studies* gives a very detailed answer to our question. After having studied carefully the processing of cheeses and the way rennet is produced, he comes to this conclusion:

> It is our considered opinion that commercial cheeses, all of them, including those in which rennet from any animal, kosher or non-kosher is used as the curdling agent, should be permitted (p. 68).

I tend to accept Rabbi Klein's decision.

I do not know exactly what process is involved in soft "French" cheese-making, but as far as I understand from Rabbi Klein's study, the basis is the same for every cheese. The difference between them is the processing time.

Rabbi Monique Susskind Goldberg
March 2005

FOR FURTHER READING

1. Graubart, Yehudah Leib, *She'eilot Uteshuvot Ḥavalim Ban'imim, Yoreh De'ah*, Part 4, No. 23 [Hebrew].

2. Grodzinsky, Ḥayyim Ozer, *Responsa Aḥiezer*, Part 2, No. 11, parag. 5 [Hebrew].

3. Klein, Isaac, *Responsa and Halakhic Studies*, second revised edition, edited by David Golinkin and Monique Susskind Goldberg, Jerusalem, 2005, pp. 53-70.

4. "Rennet", Wikipedia, http://en.wikipedia.org/wiki/Rennet.

41. Is it Permissible to Eat a Medium Rare Steak?

QUESTION

Dear Rabbi,

I have a question for you that my religion teacher couldn't answer. According to the Bible, all kinds of blood are prohibited. But are you allowed to eat a steak that's cooked medium rare?

ANSWER

For meat to be kosher, the animal is slaughtered by cutting the jugular artery and letting all the blood drain out. The meat is then rinsed and soaked in cold water for half-an-hour. After the soaking, the meat is covered with coarse salt and left for an hour on a grid or inclined board to drain whatever blood may still remain. The meat is then thoroughly rinsed (*Yoreh De'ah* 69:1, 4-6).

After this process, the meat is considered drained of the forbidden blood, and the length of cooking no longer matters.

Meat from a ritually slaughtered animal, can also be made kosher by broiling it rather than through the soaking and salting process (*ibid.* 76:1-2). However, the custom is to wash the meat and salt it immediately before broiling (*ibid.* 76:2 in the Rema). The broiling should be done on a grid which allows the blood to drip freely (*ibid.* 76:6). In this case, the meat is considered kosher when there is a change of color and a crust is formed (*ibid.* 76:4, *Taz* subparag. 9). Again, in the case of kashering by broiling, once the meat is drained of its forbidden blood, one can choose the length of cooking.

Rabbi Monique Susskind Goldberg
February 2006

FOR FURTHER READING

1. Klein, Isaac, "Broiling", in *A Guide to Jewish Religious Practice*, New York, 1992, p. 356.

2. Lipschutz, Yacov, *Kashruth*, New York, 1988, pp. 30-38.

42. May I *Kasher* Old China?

Dear Rabbi,

We recently inherited a set of family china. I have been trying to locate a serving bowl to replace one that is missing.

I found a bowl through one of the internet companies that specializes in selling replacement pieces. The piece shows no sign of wear, but is not wrapped in any way that would indicate that it has never been used. The pattern has not been made since 1984. Is there any way that we could use such a piece of china?

Also, can the glass glaze be considered as glass, and therefore not *bolei'a* [absorbent], and can it be used without kashering?

As you are not sure the bowl you found is new, you have to consider the possibility that it was used for non-kosher food.

China of ceramic and porcelain are considered earthenware, and according to *halakhah* cannot be kashered. Even with the glass glaze, the dish is considered porous (*Oraḥ Ḥayyim* 451:1, 22-23).

However, there are important contemporary decisors such as Rabbi Moshe Feinstein who allow using some pieces of china after 12 months during which they were not used. The reasons for this permission are:

1. After 12 months, the "the taste" of whatever was absorbed in the bowl has disappeared and the dish is like new (*Yoreh De'ah* 135:16).

2. Such a dish is never put directly on a flame, and thus did not absorb much of the forbidden food.

3. It is considered a substantial loss (*hefsed merubeh*) to the owner if he/she is not permitted to use valuable pieces of china. This is an argument often used for being lenient in matters related to *kashrut* (see, for example, *Orah Hayyim* 467:11).

In the specific case you mentioned, the bowl should not be used for twelve months after you acquire it, and then it should be washed. According to Rabbi Feinstein, who follows the Tur (*Yoreh De'ah* 121), you should then immerse it three times in very hot water (*hag'alah*).

Enjoy your dishes!

Rabbi Monique Susskind Goldberg
February 2005

FOR FURTHER READING

1. Ashkenazi, Tzvi Hirsch, *Hakham Tzvi*, No. 75 [Hebrew].

2. Eiger, Akiva, *Responsa Rabbi Akiva Eiger*, No. 43 [Hebrew].

3. Eisenstadt, Avraham Tzvi Hirsch, *Pithei Teshuvah* to *Yoreh De'ah* 122, subparag. 3 [Hebrew].

4. Feinstein, Moshe, *Responsa Igrot Moshe, Yoreh De'ah*, part 2, No. 46 [Hebrew].

5. Klein, Isaac, *A Guide to Jewish Religious Practice*, New York, 1992, pp. 113-114.

6. Yosef, Ovadiah, *Responsa Yabia Omer*, part 1, *Yoreh De'ah*, No. 6 [Hebrew].

43. May One Use the Same Dishwasher for Milk and Meat?

QUESTION

Dear Rabbi,

Can I use the same dishwasher for milk as well as for meat dishes?

ANSWER

A mechanical dishwasher cleans the dishes by spraying hot water on them. First, water containing a strong detergent is sprayed for cleaning the dishes; then, clean water is sprayed to remove the detergent. Some dishwashers also have additional programs like heating to dry the dishes, and pre-rinsing before the washing.

Let's suppose, for example, that you wash meat dishes followed by dairy dishes. The hot water running on the dairy dishes did not absorb the meat "taste" directly from meat, it only absorbed some of the "meat taste" that was absorbed in the walls of the dishwasher and this is not a problem (*Yoreh De'ah* 95:3). The hot water running in the dishwasher is only giving the "taste" of the meat to the dairy dish by second degree [*noten ta'am bar noten ta'am*] (*Ḥullin*, 111b). Therefore, it is permissible to use the same dishwasher for milk and meat dishes, provided you do separate cycles for milk and meat dishes.

One should, however, be sure that no piece of food remains in the dishwasher that could give a meat "taste" directly to the dairy dishes (*Yoreh De'ah* 95:3 in the Rema and 91:2). This is why some authorities (like Rabbi Moshe Feinstein) require different trays for the dishwasher (for dairy and for meat), to ensure that no piece of dairy food remains for the meat cycle (and *vice versa*).

There is another opinion, however, according to which the dish-soap that is injected in the beginning of the cycle gives to any food remaining in the dishwasher *ta'am lifgam* "a bad taste" and thus cancels the problem of "taste" given by food remaining on the trays (*Yoreh De'ah* 95:4). On this basis, Rabbi Joseph Karo even allows washing dairy and meat dishes **together** when dish soap is added to the water. But many halakhic authorities believe this leniency is acceptable only after the fact and not from the start.

In consequence, it is recommended:

– to wash the meat and dairy dishes in different cycles;
– to make sure that there are no pieces of food in the filter or on the trays when you do a new cycle;
– not to use the pre-rinsing program;
– it is not necessary to have two trays; the soap from the preceding cycle has cancelled the "taste" that was on the tray.

Rabbi Monique Susskind Goldberg
March 2007

FOR FURTHER READING

1. Feinstein, Moshe, *Responsa Igrot Moshe, Orah Hayyim*, part 1, No. 104; *Yoreh De'ah*, part 2, Nos. 28-29 and part 3, Nos. 10-11; *Orah Hayyim*, part 3, No. 58 [Hebrew].

2. Klein, Isaac, *A Guide to Jewish Religious Practice*, New York, 1992, pp. 369-370.

3. Toledano, Pinhas, *Seridim* 3 (Heshvan 5743), pp. 47-50 [Hebrew].

4. Yosef, Yitzhak, *Yalkut Yosef*, vol. 10, *Issur Veheter*, part 3, pp. 484-492 [Hebrew].

5. Zvihi, Pinhas, *Responsa Ateret Paz*, part 1, vol. 2, *Yoreh De'ah*, No. 4 [Hebrew].

44. Does Wine Made by Non-Jews Render the Vessels That It Touches Non-Kosher?

QUESTION

Dear Rabbi,

Are the vessels that came into contact with wine made by non-Jews *treif*?

ANSWER

One should distinguish between two categories of wine made by non-Jews:

1. *Yain Nesekh*, wine which was dedicated to idolatry.

It is forbidden for a Jew to drink from it or to benefit from it (Deuteronomy 32:38; *Avodah Zarah* 29b and 62a; Maimonides, Laws of Forbidden Foods 11:1). Such a wine is considered inherently impure and is therefore forbidden and can render the glass or utensil that it touches impure (*Avodah Zarah* 30b; Maimonides, Laws of Other Fathers of Uncleanness 6:8).

However, nowadays, most non-Jews are not idol-worshippers (this was already the opinion of the Rema in *Yoreh De'ah* 124:24; see also above, No. 26) and idolatry involving wine libation is not known in our area. Therefore, it is not likely that such a wine would ever be in contact with dishes in a private Jewish home.

2. *Stam Yeinam*, wine made by non-Jews for consumption.

The authorities also forbid Jews to drink such a wine (see Maimonides, Laws of Forbidden Foods 11:3; *Yoreh De'ah* 123:1; Naḥmanides, *Ḥidushei Haramban, Avodah Zarah* 36b).

a. In the sources, the original motivation for the prohibition of wine made by non-Jews was to prevent mixed marriages (see for instance *Avodah Zarah* 36b; *Shabbat* 17b). Like bread and oil, the Sages believed that buying wine made by non-Jews would increase the opportunities to socialize with them and lead to intermarriage.

In the case of cooking by non-Jews, the authorities were divided on the question whether this food would render the utensils not kosher (*Yoreh De'ah* 113:16). We are of the opinion that the utensils are not included in this enactment. In consequence, the vessels in contact with wine made by non-Jews do not become unkosher.

b. Another reason wine made by non-Jews could be forbidden by the authorities is the suspicion that non-kosher products were used in the process.

This is not the place to elaborate on the process of wine-making. For our purpose, suffice it to mention that one of the steps in wine-making is clarifying the wine. In some wineries, the product used to clarify the wine, the fining agent, is not kosher and therefore, even if the quantity that remains in the wine is minimal, the wine is still considered unkosher by a great number of authorities.

However, some important halakhic authorities were lenient regarding the use of non-kosher fining products in alcoholic drinks. Rabbi Ezekiel Landau (the *Noda Bi-Yehudah*, 1713-1793), for example, allows the use of a fining agent made from non-kosher fish for clearing a kind of beer. His reason for being lenient is that the intention, when the fining agent was added, was only to clear the beer and no taste remained from the fining agent in the drink.

In contemporary times, R. Moshe Feinstein uses this same argument in two of his responsa, in order to allow using non-kosher products to make candy glazes and certain vinegars.

In conclusion:

1. *Stam Yeinam*, wine made by non-Jews for consumption, is not unkosher in and of itself.

2. The decree to prohibit wine made by non-Jews to avoid intermarriage was established only on the wine and did not include the vessels in contact with the wine.

For those reasons, the vessels that come in contact with wine made by non-Jews do not become *treif*.

Rabbi Monique Susskind Goldberg
September 2005

FOR FURTHER READING

1. Dorff, Elliot, "The Use of All Wines", *Responsa 1980-1990*, New York, 2005, pp. 295-318 also available at: www.rabbinicalassembly.org/teshuvot/docs/1986-1990/dorff_wines.pdf

2. *Entziklopedia Talmudit*, vol. 24, Jerusalem, 1999, "*Yain Nesekh*", columns 283-330; "*Yayin Shel Goyim*" columns 330-445 [Hebrew].

3. Feinstein, Moshe, *Responsa Igrot Moshe, Yoreh De'ah* part 2, Nos. 24, 36 [Hebrew].

4. For a discussion whether Christianity should be considered idolatry, see above, No. 26.

5. Landau, Yeḥezkel, *Noda Bi-Yehudah, Mahadurah Kama, Yoreh De'ah*, No. 26 [Hebrew].

6. Silverman, Israel Nissan, "*B'Inyan Stam Yeinam Shel Goyyim*", *Conservative Judaism* 18:2 (Winter, 1964), pp. 1-5 [Hebrew] = "Are All Wines Kosher?" in: Seymour Siegel and Elliot Gertel, eds., *Conservative Judaism and Jewish Law*, New York, 1977, pp. 308-316. Both were reprinted in David Golinkin, editor, *Proceedings of the Committee on Jewish Law and Standards of the Conservative Movement 1927-1970*, Vol. 3, Jerusalem, 1997, pp. 1300-1313.

45. Is the Blood of Fish Prohibited?

QUESTION

Dear Rabbi,

I am a Gentile. I understand that fish blood is prohibited. If I accidentally ate fish blood, can I repent and atone for my sin?

ANSWER

The blood of fish is not forbidden by the laws of *Kashrut* [Jewish dietary laws]. The prohibition regarding eating food with blood applies only to wild animals such as deer, domesticated animals such as cows and sheep, and fowl. These are the animals that require *shehitah* [ritual slaughtering] (see *Yoreh De'ah* 66:1, based on *Keritot* 21b).

Though non-Jews are are not required to obey all of the commandments in the Torah, they are supposed to observe the seven Noahide laws (see above, No. 30). However, the Noahide Laws do not include the prohibition of eating blood and, in any case, fish blood is not included in this prohibiton. Therefore, the fact that you ate fish blood does not require repentance.

Sincerely,
Rabbi Diana Villa
March 2003

46. Is Royal Jelly Kosher?

QUESTION

Dear Rabbi,

Is Royal Jelly to be considered kosher like honey, or is it not kosher because it is made by the bees?

ANSWER

In beehives, two kinds of substances are created by the worker bees.

a) Honey is created by bees as a food source. In cold weather, or when food sources are scarce, bees use the stored honey as their source of energy.

The worker bees raise larvae and collect the nectar that will become honey in the hive. Leaving the hive, they collect sugar-rich flower nectar and return. In the hive, the bees use their "honey stomachs" to ingest and regurgitate the nectar a number of times until it is partially digested. The bees work together as a group until the product reaches a desired quality. It is then stored in honeycomb cells.

b) Royal Jelly is a honey bee secretion that is used in the nutrition of the larvae. It is secreted from glands in the heads of young workers and used (among other substances) to feed all of the larvae in the colony, including those destined to become workers. If a queen bee is needed, a larva is chosen and will receive **only** royal jelly, and in large quantities, as its food source for the first four days of its growth, and this rapid, early feeding triggers the development of queen morphology, including the fully developed ovaries needed to lay eggs.

Normally, the laws of *kashrut* do not allow us to eat any product derived from a non-kosher animal, based on the rule that "what derives from an impure [animal] is impure" [*hayotzei min hatamei – tamei*] (see *Bekhorot* 7b).

However, bee honey is allowed (*Yoreh De'ah* 81:8). In the sources, there are two explanations for this permission:

Some early Sages [*tannaim*] thought that the bees just suck the nectar from the flowers and then process it; i.e., honey is not something produced by the body of the insect itself. It seems that classical Jewish sources were not aware of the process the nectar goes through in the hive, and related to honey as a product that derives only from flower nectar.

Others claim that it is a *gezeirat hakatuv*, a special biblical decree. In this case, the Sages learn from the verse in Lev 11:21 that although it is forbidden to eat insects and anything produced by insects, bee honey is an exception and is allowed (see *Bekhorot, ibid.*).

As Royal Jelly is very bitter by itself, it is sold diluted in honey. Most authorities allow Royal Jelly, seeing no reason to distinguish between it and honey, especially since it has potential health benefits (see Rabbi Eliezer Waldenberg, *Tzitz Eliezer*, part 11, No. 59 and part 12, No. 54; Rabbi Yitzḥak Yosef, *Yalkut Yosef* on *Yoreh De'ah* 81, parag. 40, vol. 9, pp. 159-162).

Some halakhic authorities, invoking the particularly bitter taste of Royal Jelly, allow its use diluted in honey, as it is usually sold. They use the argument of *noten ta'am lifgam*. When a substance imparts a disgusting flavor to food, it does not render that food unkosher even if the substance itself is not kosher (see *Yoreh De'ah* 103:1 and *Tzitz Eliezer, ibid.*).

In Israel, Royal Jelly diluted in honey (1/40 the amount of honey) is sold with a *hekhsher* [stamp indicating it is kosher]. There is, however, a note that one should consult one's rabbi about eating it.

Since most authorities allow it because it has potential health benefits, we believe you have a strong case to consider Royal Jelly kosher.

Shabbat Shalom and Happy Shavu'ot!

Rabbi Diana Villa
June 2008

FOR FURTHER READING

1. About Honey and Royal jelly:
   http://animals.nationalgeographic.com/animals/bugs/honeybee.html
   http://animals.about.com/od/bees/f/royaljelly.htm

2. Blech, Zushe Yosef, *Kosher Food Production*, second edition, Iowa, 2008, pp. 376-382.

3. *Entziklopedia Talmudit*, vol. 7, Jerusalem 1956, *Devash*, columns 197-198 [Hebrew].

4. Klein, Ḥayyim, *Kashrut Hadevash Le'akhilah*, Kiryat Arba-Hevron, December 2007 also available at:
   http://rabanim.org/ index.php ?option=com_content& task=view& id=215&Itemid=49 [Hebrew].

5. Klein, Isaac, *A Guide to Jewish Religious Practice*, New York, 1992, pp. 375-376.

6. Melamed, Israel, *Likutim Bekhashrut*, Beth El Yeshivah, February, 2008 also available at: http://www.yeshiva.org.il/ midrash/shiur.asp?cat=935&id=7173&q=דבש [Hebrew].

47. What Makes Bread Kosher?

QUESTION

Dear Rabbi,

What is the difference between a "kosher" bakery and a regular bakery? I understand that a kosher butcher must follow strict laws in slaughtering animals, but what does that have to do with a kosher bakery?

ANSWER

In the *Mishnah* (*Avodah Zarah* 2:6), there is a list of foods prepared by non-Jews and forbidden to Jews and bread is on the list. The Talmud (*Avodah Zarah* 35b) gives two reasons for this: to avoid eating non-kosher food and to avoid intermarriage.

Regarding the first point, you must be aware that bread is not only made from flour, and even if you do buy bread from a "regular" bakery, you should buy bread with the ingredients clearly written on the package, to ensure that no non-kosher ingredients, such as animal fat, were used in the baking of the bread. Usually the breads in health food stores use only vegetarian ingredients. To avoid buying bread containing non-kosher ingredients, people who keep kosher prefer to buy their bread in a kosher bakery or they buy mass-produced bread with a kashrut symbol such as OU, OK. etc.

The other reason is an old custom, from the time of the *Mishnah* and Talmud, not to eat bread, oil or wine made by non-

Jews, in order to prevent a lot of joint meals which might lead to intermarriage. Since that time, numerous halakhic authorities have ruled that it is permissible in certain situations to buy bread in non-Jewish bakeries (see *Yoreh De'ah* 112:1-16). However, it still remains a very strong custom in the Orthodox world not to eat bread made by non-Jews. This is why an Orthodox Jew will only buy bread baked in a kosher bakery or bearing a kashrut symbol.

Rabbi Monique Susskind Goldberg
January 2003

FOR FURTHER READING

Lipschutz, Yacov, *Kashruth*, New York, 1988, pp. 61-63.

LIFE CYCLE

48. Must One Be Circumcised in Order to Be Called Up to the Torah?
If a Jewish Man Was Not Circumcised as an Infant, How Should He Be Circumcised?

QUESTION

Dear Rabbi,

A friend of mine asked me if an uncircumcised Jewish man is recognized as a Jew. I know that uncircumcised men are not allowed to get an *aliyah* or to perform any ritual connected with the service, but aren't they still sons of Jewish mothers?

If an uncircumcised Jew decides to get circumcised as an adult later in his life, must he be circumcised by a *mohel*? Another friend's son was circumcised by a doctor rather than a *mohel* – what does the tradition have to say about this? Would you please mention some references (Talmud, *Responsa*, etc.) so that we can take a deeper look into this topic.

ANSWER

According to *halakhah*, a person is Jewish if his/her mother is Jewish (see *Kiddushin* 68b; *Even Ha'ezer* 8:5) or if he/she converted to Judaism.

> Circumcision does not "make" a person Jewish, for he is Jewish already by birth. The circumcision rather testifies that he who bears this sign sealed in his flesh is under the covenant... Through the covenant, he is bound to all of the Children of Israel, and through them to God (R. Hershel Matt quoted by R. Isaac Klein).

However, the rite of circumcision is central in Judaism, as circumcision is the sign of the covenant (*brit*) between God and the Jewish people (Genesis 17:9-13). Accordingly, Jewish Law requires that every Jewish male be circumcised (*Yoreh De'ah* 260:1). If he was not circumcised by his father when he was a

143

child, then he is obligated to have himself circumcised as an adult (*ibid.* 261:1). The Bible states that if a Jewish man does not observe the commandment of circumcision, he is "cut off from his people" (Genesis 17:14). If a Jewish man was not circumcised for a good, objective reason (e.g., he was brought up in the Soviet Union and circumcision was not possible), he may have an *aliyah*. But if he is living in Israel or in a Diaspora community with many Jews and he intentionally refuses to have himself circumcised, he shows that he does not accept the covenant. There is, therefore, no point in him giving him an *aliyah* or any other honor in the synagogue.

As for your second question, according to *halakhah*, any Jew is allowed to do the circumcision (*Yoreh De'ah* 264:1). This is why the circumcision could be done by a physician if he is Jewish and knows the special procedure of the circumcision and the required blessings (it cannot merely be a surgical procedure). It is better if a rabbi is present. However, it is recommended that the circumcision be done by a *mohel* who is experienced and knowledgeable in the procedure of the circumcision and in the blessings accompanying it. A circumcision performed as surgery or by a gentile physician is not valid. If it was done in such a way, a drop of blood has to be drawn afterward by a *mohel* or a Rabbi in order to render the circumcision valid (*ibid.* in the Rema).

Sincerely,
Rabbi Monique Susskind Goldberg
April 2004

FOR FURTHER READING

1. Felder, Gedalia, *Yesodei Yeshurun*, vol. 2, New York, 1957, pp. 208-210 [Hebrew].

2. Freehof, Solomon, in: Walter Jacob, ed., *American Reform Responsa*, New York, 1983, No. 34.

3. Klein, Isaac, "Ritual Circumcision", in: *A Guide to Jewish Religious Practice*, New York, 1992, pp. 420-432.

49. What Are the Laws and Customs Regarding Baby Naming?

QUESTION

I would like some clarifications about giving a Hebrew name to a baby:

1. When do the baby boy and baby girl receive their Hebrew names?

2. Can the name of any relative be given?

3. How is she/he called to the Torah if the father is not Jewish?

ANSWER

1a. Naming a Baby Boy

A Jewish baby boy is named as part of the rite of circumcision, on the eighth day of his life, or later (if the ritual is postponed for a medical reason). This custom is recorded in the late first/early second century in the Gospel of Luke (1:59 and 2:21) and in the eighth-century *midrash* entitled *Pirkei Derabi Eliezer* in reference to Moses (chapter 48). It was also an established part of the ceremony in the ninth century (it appears in Geonic times in *Seder Rav Amram Ga'on, Seder Milah*, ed. Goldschmidt, p. 179).

Abraham, as the first Jew, whose name was changed from Abram to Abraham at the time of his circumcision, became the prototype for all male Jews (see *Tzitz Eliezer*, part 18, No. 54, based on medieval sources). Usually, the *mohel* (the man who performs the circumcision) names the child during the circumcision ritual.

1b. Naming a Baby Girl

There is no fixed practice as to when a baby girl is named. A common Ashkenazic practice today is that she receives her name when a parent gets an *aliyah* to the Torah on the Shabbat following the child's birth. The reasons for naming her when the Torah is read include: 1) that many people are present and therefore the name she will use for all ritual purposes (such as in

145

her marriage document) will be known to all; 2) that on the same occasion the mother is blessed and wished a full recovery; 3) we have an "extra soul" on Shabbat, and therefore it is the proper day to give the baby girl the name that represents her essence (see *Responsa Mishneh Halakhot*, part 13, No. 190).

Some rabbis recommend naming a baby girl on the first day the Torah is read after birth; some recommend waiting 5 days (but if Shabbat is after 3 days, it can be done then). Others recommend not to do so on the Shabbat right after birth; since the mother may not be present, one should wait for the following Shabbat. In any case, the name should be given within the first month. All of the customs have precedents and they are all valid customs (see *Responsa Mishneh Halakhot, ibid.* and part 6, No. 254; *Responsa Betzel Haḥokhmah*, part 5, No. 145; *Tzitz Eliezer*, part 13, No. 20 and the articles by Rabbi Golinkin who describes twenty different customs).

In recent years, ceremonies to mark a baby girl's birth are more common. These are called *simḥat bat, zeved habat* and in modern Israel even *britah*. The ceremony marks the baby girl's entry into the Jewish people, just as circumcision marks a boy's entry into the covenant. The Hebrew name is often given at this time in non-Orthodox ceremonies, instead of when one of the parents gets an *aliyah* (see for instance *Moreh Derekh*, pp. A-23 and A-44).

2. Naming a Child after a Relative

Rabbi Isaac Klein summarizes the prevalent customs: Ashkenazic Jews usually name a child after deceased relatives, while Sephardim also name it after living relatives.

When the child is named after a relative of the opposite sex, the closest equivalent name in the correct gender is chosen. This is all based on custom; there is no normative regulation.

3. Name of a Child whose Father is Not Jewish

Traditionally a child's name includes his father's name, for example, Reuben the son of Jacob. In non-Orthodox circles, it is common to use both the father's and the mother's Hebrew names, for example, Reuben the son of Jacob and Leah. However, if the father is not Jewish, Conservative practice is to use only the mother's name.

Rabbi Diana Villa
June 2007

FOR FURTHER READING

1. *Entziklopedia Talmudit*, vol. 4, Jerusalem, 1956, *Brit Milah*, column 256 [Hebrew].

2. Goldin, Hyman, *Hamadrikh*, New York, 1939, pp. 35-36.

3. Golinkin, David, "When Should Baby Girls Be Named?", *Insight Israel*, second series, Jerusalem, 2006, pp. 220-225 and the longer Hebrew version found in: *Studies in Memory of Prof. Zev Falk*, Jerusalem, 2005, pp. 27-38 [Hebrew].

4. Klein, Isaac, *A Guide to Jewish Religious Practice*, New York, 1992, p. 429.

5. Rank, Perry and Freeman, Gordon, eds., *Moreh Derekh: The Rabbinical Assembly Rabbi's Manual*, New York, 1998, pp. A-23 and A-44.

50. What Is the Halakhic Status of a Child Born with the Help of a Non-Jewish Surrogate Mother?

QUESTION

Dear Rabbi,

I am interested in a Conservative ruling on the following: Since it would be dangerous for my wife to carry a child, our non-Jewish sister-in-law has carried our baby as a surrogate mother. Since we are both Jewish, it is hard for us to accept that the child conceived by our own eggs and sperm, who is genetically our child, may have to convert. Besides, my sister-in-law acted out of love, and my wife considers it offensive to say that her carrying our son in her uterus somehow tainted him and stripped him of his Jewishness.

Does our baby require conversion? What would the consequences be if we did not convert him?

ANSWER

A baby's Jewishness is determined by the birth mother, no matter whether the genetic material that impregnated her was Jewish or not.

The Talmud discusses a case in which two twin brothers were conceived while the mother was a gentile, but were born after she converted. Both brothers were considered Jewish (*Yevamot* 97b and *Yoreh De'ah* 269:4).

The decisors ruled on this basis that "If a non-Jewish woman converts when she is pregnant, her child does not require immersion (*Yoreh De'ah* 268:6)". This proves that it is the status of the birth mother that determines the baby's status; if she had not converted, the child would not be considered Jewish (see *Mishnah Kiddushin* 3:12). Most authorities agree with this position and therefore require conversion for a child born from a non-Jewish surrogate mother.

Some additional considerations regarding who is considered the mother include that a fetus is considered "part of the mother" (*Ḥullin* 58a) and not an independent entity. In addition, the embryo in the first forty days is "mere fluid" (*Yevamot* 69b) and the embryo is transferred to the surrogate mother in the first few days.

The fact that your sister-in-law carried the baby was an act of love for both of you. Nevertheless, under Jewish law since she is not Jewish, the child is not considered Jewish.

You should not worry about the baby's conversion process; it is a very easy procedure. It includes circumcision (which the baby would undergo in any case) and immersion, and, unless the child expresses his disagreement as soon as he turns 13, he is automatically Jewish. If he is not converted as a baby and you are honest with the child regarding his birth circumstances and he were to meet a Conservative or Orthodox woman that he wished to marry, he would then find himself in the uncomfortable situation of having to convert as an adult in order to marry her. A distressful situation can be avoided by his undergoing the procedure as a baby.

Mazal Tov on the impending birth of your child!

Sincerely,
Rabbi Diana Villa
April 2006

FOR FURTHER READING

1. Bleich, David, "In Vitro Fertilization: Maternal Identity and Conversion" in: *Contemporary Halakhic Problems*, vol. 4, New York, 1995, pp. 237-272.

2. Feldman, David M., *Health and Medicine in the Jewish Tradition*, New York, 1986, pp. 72-74.

3. Goldberg, Zalman Nehemiah, *Tehumin* 5 (1984), pp. 248-259 [Hebrew].

4. Jacob, Walter, ed., *American Reform Responsa*, New York, 1983, pp. 505-507.

5. Kilav, Abraham Isaac Halevi, *Tehumin* 5 (1984), pp. 260-267 [Hebrew].

6. Mackler, Aaron in: Aaron Mackler, ed., *Life and Death Responsibilities in Jewish Biomedical Ethics*, New York, 2000, pp. 174-187 = *Responsa 1991-2000*, edited by Kassel Abelson and David Fine, New York, 2002, pp. 137-145 = http://www.rabbinicalassembly.org/law/teshuvot_public.html, under *Yoreh De'ah*, Conversion.

7. Steinberg, Avraham, *Entziklopedia Hilkhatit Refu'it*, vol. 2, Jerusalem, 1991, cols. 129-138 [Hebrew].

MARRIAGE

51. May a *Kohen* Marry a Convert?

QUESTION

Dear Rabbi,

Could you tell me how severe is the prohibition of a *kohen* marrying a convert? Is it a Biblical or a Rabbinic prohibition? If one marries anyway, despite the prohibition, what are the repercussions?

ANSWER

According to Leviticus 21:7, marriage of a *kohen* to a *zonah* (harlot) is forbidden (and cf. Maimonides, Laws of Marriage 1:7; *Even Ha'ezer* 6:1). The Talmud considered all non-Jewish women to be of questionable character; therefore the Sages expanded the definition of a *zonah* to a convert as well (see *Mishnah Yevamot* 6:5 and *Yevamot* 60b-61b; Maimonides, Laws of Forbidden Sexual Relations 18:1).

This is why a converted woman is considered unfit to become the wife of a *kohen* (see Maimonides, *ibid.* 18:3; *Even Ha'Ezer* 6:8), and Maimonides (*ibid.* 19:6) adds that the children of such a union would lose their priestly status and become *ḥallalim.*[4]

Even though such a marriage is forbidden, this is a rabbinic and not a biblical prohibition (see *Ḥidushei Haritba* to *Yevamot* 76a). Therefore, some rabbinic authorities who forbid such a union nonetheless allow other options.

Rabbi David Zvi Hoffmann was asked about a non-Jew who was married by civil law to a *kohen*; they had a child who was circumcised and subsequently died. The woman wanted to convert and be Jewish, like her deceased son, and there was a risk of her becoming insane if she wasn't allowed to do so. Rabbi Hoffmann allowed the conversion. Since rabbinic law forbids marriage in these cases (but not **non-marital** cohabitation) he ruled

---

4   They cannot fulfill the functions of a *kohen*, such as getting the first *aliyah* to the Torah, blessing the congregation, leading the recitation of *Birkat Hamazon* and redeeming the firstborn.

that they should remain married under civil law but not have a Jewish wedding. Any children they might have would be *hallalim* (*Responsa Melamed Le-Ho'il*, part 3, No. 8).

In our day, we cannot trace the status of *kohanim* back to the Second Temple period (they are only **presumed** to be *kohanim*). Furthermore, converts do not come from an idolatrous society and therefore do not lack moral integrity, as it was presumed in Talmudic times. It follows that continuing this prohibition is a *Hillul Hashem* (a desecration of God's name or of His Torah) because it implies that we relate to members of other monotheistic religions as morally loose people.

On this basis, Rabbi Isaac Klein allowed a Conservative rabbi to perform such weddings, though the children would become *hallalim*. Rabbi Arnold Goodman reaffirmed this position in 1996, but added that the children of such unions would **not** be considered *hallalim*.

Most Conservative rabbis will perform weddings between a *kohen* and a convert, and if you come on *aliyah* you could register as a married couple based on your civil marriage.

Sincerely,
Rabbi Diana Villa
January 2003

FOR FURTHER READING

1. Goodman, Arnold, "Solemnizing a Marriage between a Cohen and a Convert", in: *Responsa 1991-2000*, edited by Kassel Abelson and David Fine, New York, 2002, pp. 599-601.

2. Klein, Isaac, "The Marriage of a *Kohen* to a *Giyoret*", *Proceedings of the Rabbinical Assembly* 32 (1968), pp. 219-223, reprinted in Isaac Klein, *Responsa and Halakhic Studies*, second revised and expanded edition, edited by David Golinkin and Monique Susskind Goldberg, Jerusalem, 2005, pp. 27-32.

52. May a *Kohen* Marry a Divorcee?

QUESTION

Dear Rabbi,

I am a *kohen* (at least my father said so), and I wonder how severe is the prohibition against marrying a divorcee? Are the laws as currently applied Biblical or Rabbinic, and does this distinction make a difference?

ANSWER

There is a clear Biblical prohibition against the marriage of a *kohen* and a divorcee: "They shall not marry a woman defiled by harlotry, nor shall they marry one divorced from her husband" (Leviticus 21:7).

According to *halakhah*, a *kohen* who marries a divorcee must divorce her (see *Even Ha'ezer* 6:1 and Maimonides, Laws of Forbidden Sexual Relations 17:2).

Even though such a marriage is prohibited, it is valid after the fact (Maimonides, *ibid.* 17:1; *Even Ha'ezer, ibid.*). However, the *kohen* who marries a divorcee loses his priestly privileges such as the right to bless the people with the Priestly Blessing or to go up first to the Torah (see Maimonides, *ibid.* 17:1; *Orah Hayyim* 128:40). The children of such a union are legitimate but are *hallalim* (see above, p. 151, note 4); they cannot fulfill the functions of a *kohen* (see *Even Ha'ezer* 7:12).

There are three halakhic solutions to this dilemma:

1. When a *kohen* wants to marry a divorcee, some authorities recommend investigating the particular case to determine whether the woman's first marriage was valid. If, for instance, there was a problem with the witnesses, the first marriage can be annulled, the woman can be considered single and there is thus no impediment for her to marry a *kohen* (see Rabbi Ovadiah Yosef, *Responsa Yabi'ah Omer*, part 8, *Even Ha'ezer*, Nos. 5, 7).

2. Living together as common law partners:

Living in a committed monogamous relationship without marriage would not transgress Torah law, as opposed to marrying which, as we have seen above, is a Biblical prohibition.

Rabbi Moshe Feinstein point outs that the harsh rulings (flogging and forcing to divorce) apply only when the *kohen* is **married** to a divorcee, not when they merely live together (*Igrot Moshe, Even Ha'ezer*, part 1, No. 5). We could conclude on this basis, that a *kohen* could live with a divorced woman as his common law wife.

This arrangement is called *pilagshut* [concubinage] in Jewish Law. As we learn in *Sanhedrin* 21b: "What are 'wives', and what are 'concubines'? – Rav Judah said in Rav's name: Wives have *ketubah* and *kiddushin*, concubines have neither" (cf. Rabbi Diana Villa listed below). This is equivalent to a common law relationship that can be officially registered in countries where this status provides legal rights. If this is not possible, a contract should be drawn or a civil marriage should be performed to cover the rights of each partner.

3. Declaring that marriage between a *kohen* and a divorcee is permitted in our day.

Indeed, two Conservative responsa favor the third approach.

A. According to Deuteronomy 24:1, a man can divorce his wife when he finds something unseemly [*ervat davar*] in her. Rabbis Bokser and Friedman understand that this was the reason a *kohen* could not marry a divorcee. A *kohen* who served God in the Temple could not be associated with a woman with a doubtful past. However, being divorced is not considered a blemish in our times; most divorces are due to incompatibility and have no connection to any unseemly conduct. Therefore they conclude that there is no problem for a *kohen* to marry a divorcee.

In their opinion, a *kohen* in our times is only **presumed** to be a *kohen* as he cannot trace his ancestry back to the Second Temple period and his role in Jewish law has been

154

diminished (see *Responsa Ribash*, No. 94). They add that a *kohen* marrying a divorcee should relinquish his status as a *kohen* (saying the priestly blessing, getting the first *aliyah* to the Torah, leading when saying grace and redeeming the firstborn), which they believe he would readily be willing to do.

On the basis of all these reasons, Rabbis Bokser and Friedman allow a marriage between a *kohen* and a divorcee. Yet in deference to the traditional rejection of such weddings, they propose that only a small wedding should take place.

B. The second responsum is based on the fact that in certain circumstances, the rabbis in the Talmud permitted the cancellation of a Biblical prohibition (*la'akor davar min ha-Torah* = to uproot a biblical commandment).

According to the Talmud, a *Beit Din* (rabbinic court) has the authority to uproot a biblical law in three instances (see *Yevamot* 89a-90b):

1) When the Rabbis rule that a certain commandment should not be performed (*shev ve'al ta'aseh*). For example, it is a Rabbinic enactment not to blow the *shofar* on Rosh Hashanah if it coincides with Shabbat, even though according to the Torah it should be blown. The Rabbis wanted to ensure that the *shofar* would not be carried in the public domain on Shabbat (see *Yevamot* 90b).

2) The Rabbis can uproot a Biblical commandment when the issue is monetary (*davar shebemamon*), since Rabbinic courts have the authority to confiscate property (*hefker beit din hefker*). The example given is the annulment of marriage based on the *Beit Din*'s confiscation of the money given by the husband to the bride to effect the betrothal (nowadays a ring), which is retroactively not considered the husband's property, and therefore the betrothal becomes invalid (*ibid.*).

3) In certain circumstances, the Rabbis rule that we should actively violate a specific prohibition (*kum aseh*), because of the demands of the moment (*hora'at sha'ah*). The example

quoted is Elijah sacrificing on Mt. Carmel (I Kings 18), even though according to the Bible it was forbidden to sacrifice outside the Temple. The Talmud defines this as *lemigdar milta*, a special exception to keep the Jews away from idolatry (*ibid.*).

Although there is a Biblical prohibition [*issur de-Oraita*] against a *kohen* marrying a divorcee, Rabbi Arnold Goodman considers that we are in a time of crisis due to intermarriage and the high divorce rate, and it is highly probable that a *kohen* seeking to marry will meet a divorcee. There is a risk that if he is not allowed to marry a divorcee, he may end up marrying a non-Jew. Therefore, because of the demand of the moment [*hora'at sha'ah*], he concludes that we can uproot a Biblical commandment in this particular case and permit rabbis to perform such a wedding.

Rabbi Goodman explains that rabbis in every generation have the biblical authority to uproot a biblical law. He bases this opinion on a commentary by the Rashba:

> It was not a matter of the Sages deciding on their own to uproot a matter of the Torah, but it is one of the *mitzvot* in the Torah to obey the 'judges in your day' (Deuteronomy 17:9) and anything they see necessary to permit is permissible from the Torah (*Ḥidushei Harashba, Nedarim* 90b).

According to the Torah, the Sages of every generation have the authority to change Torah law, even by uprooting it. In this case, the Rabbis can uproot the Biblical law and allow a *kohen* to marry a divorcee.

In Rabbi Goodman's opinion, the *kohen* does not have to relinquish his status as *kohen* and the wedding may be celebrated publicly.

In our opinion, actively uprooting a Biblical prohibition is an extreme measure. The Rashba's justification appears in his commentary on the Talmud and it is not clear that he meant to rule that Rabbinic authorities can still take such extreme measures. It is doubtful that any Rabbinic body in our days has such far-reaching authority. In addition, in this particular case, we do not consider that the situation justifies a temporary abrogation of a specific prohibition. The situation affects only a small segment of the Jewish population, and even in those cases, as we have indicated above, there are other solutions available.

On the other hand, we could accept Bokser and Friedman's argument in the first Conservative *responsum*. Because of the uncertainty regarding the genealogy of *kohanim*, changing circumstances regarding their status and their limited ritual function on the one hand and the rejection of a blemished status for a divorcee on the other hand, allowing unions between a *kohen* and a divorcee should not be considered uprooting a Biblical commandment.

Nonetheless, since the marriage of a *kohen* to a divorcee is forbidden in traditional *halakhah*, priestly privileges should be rescinded.

This *responsum* could be adopted by those couples who reject the option of *pilagshut*, of living together as a common law couple without formalizing their union.

Sincerely,
Rabbi Diana Villa
January 2003

FOR FURTHER READING

1. Bokser, Ben-Zion and Friedman, Theodore, "Marrying a Kohen and a Divorced Woman", *Proceedings of the Rabbinical Assembly* 18 (1954), pp. 55-58 reprinted in David Golinkin, ed., *Proceedings of the Committee on Jewish Law and Standards of the Conservative Movement 1927-1970*, Jerusalem, 1997, vol. 3, pp. 1459-1462.

2. Goodman, Arnold, "Solemnizing the Marriage between a Kohen and a Divorcee" in: *Responsa 1991-2000*, edited by Kassel Abelson and David Fine, New York, 2002, pp. 593-598.

3. Villa, Diana, "Concubinage", in: Monique Susskind Goldberg and Diana Villa, *Za'akat Dalot: Halakhic Solutions for the Agunot*

of Our Time, Jerusalem, 2006, pp. 205-234 [Hebrew with an English summary on pp. xxi-xxii].

53. How Can One Prevent the *Agunah* Problem Before Getting Married?

QUESTION

Dear Rabbi,

I am an American Jew currently planning for my wedding in June. I have done a lot of research on the problem of Israeli and American *agunot* (women whose husbands refuse to give them the Jewish writ of divorce) and I would like to try to prevent this problem from ever happening to me. Besides a "Lieberman clause", what can I add to my *ketubah* and/or other wedding documents to facilitate any *get* process that might occur later, either in America or in Israel?

ANSWER

According to *halakhah*, it is the husband who divorces his wife and he must do so of his own free will: a *get* (Jewish divorce document) given against the husband's will is called *get me'useh* and is usually invalid. The woman remains a married woman (*eshet ish*). She cannot remarry and, if she has children from another man, they will be considered *mamzerim* (they and their descendants will be forbidden to marry other Jews unless they too are *mamzerim* themselves or converts). In many cases, the husband takes advantage of the power given to him by Jewish law to prevent the wife from receiving the *get*. He does this out of revenge or in order to extort property from his wife or force her to give him child custody. As we mentioned above, as long as the husband does not give her the *get*, she cannot remarry, even though she and her husband no longer live together any more as husband and wife.

The Center for Women in Jewish Law at the Schechter Institute of Jewish Studies published *Za'akat Dalot: Halakhic Solutions for the Agunot of Our Time* in 2006, in which we studied this issue in depth.

We do not recommend the use of the Lieberman clause, since it only commits the couple to come before a *Beit Din* (rabbinic court) for arbitration in case they wish to divorce. This cannot be enforced, and even if the couple agrees to come to the *Beit Din*, it provides no incentive for the husband to give a *get*, relying only on his good will, which is not very helpful in cases of recalcitrance.

There are two other preventive methods that you can apply:

1. **Conditional marriage:** This consists of signing a document in the rabbi's study just before the wedding, that says that if you should separate and if, six months after the civil divorce is obtained the husband still refuses to give a *get*, the marriage would be annulled retroactively. If the husband agrees to give the *get*, the marriage will be considered valid and there will be no reason to annul it. Under the *ḥuppah* [Jewish marriage canopy], the rabbi will tell the couple they are marrying according to the laws of Moses and Israel and the conditions they agreed to before. There is a standard text (see Bohnen and Klein listed below) to be used for these occasions. It is important that if the text is changed in any way, care should be taken to ensure that it is still valid under Jewish law.

    The marriage's annulment does not affect the status of the children; they would be considered children of unwed parents and could later marry any Jew of their choice. Children are *mamzerim*, according to Jewish Law, only if their mother had been previously married and gave birth to them before she obtained a Jewish writ of divorce.

    Unfortunately, even though this solution has been around since the fifteenth century and is being reconsidered both in Israeli and American modern Orthodox circles and has been used by Conservative rabbis since 1968, it has not been widely accepted as a valid halakhic solution yet. Therefore, should you come to Israel and the U.S. Joint *Beit Din* of the Conservative Movement had already annulled the marriage or were you to present the document with the condition to the local rabbinate here in order for them to annul the marriage, it wouldn't be accepted (at least for the time being).[5]

    (For more information see *Za'akat Dalot* listed below, chapter 3).

5   Some Orthodox couples are currently signing such agreements at the Center for Women's Justice in Israel.

2. **Prenuptial agreement:** There are different versions of prenuptial agreements that are used by Orthodox and Conservative rabbis in the U.S. and Israel. Their purpose is to pressure the husband by forcing him to pay a large sum of money as long as he refuses to give the *get*. The agreement has to be written by an authority who understands Jewish law, to make sure it doesn't even mention the *get* or invalidate the divorce (since the husband has to give the *get* of his own free will). It is usually presented as a high alimony sum, or financial support that must continue as long as the marriage is still valid (i.e. there has been no *get*). The agreement must be legalized by a court or notary public before the wedding, and in Israel it is recommended that it be taken to the civil courts to be implemented. When this happens, the husband will presumably go to the rabbinic courts and give the *get* to get out of these financial liabilities.

(For more information see *Za'akat Dalot*, chapter 1 and *To Learn and To Teach* listed below).

Let us hope that the situation in which you might need these solutions never arises. However, considering the real problem many women have with recalcitrant husbands, you are smart to ensure this does not happen to you.

Mazal Tov on your upcoming wedding and please write us again should you require further details.

Rabbi Diana Villa
April 2004

FOR FURTHER READING

1. Bohnen, Eli *et al*, *"T'nai B'kiddushin"*, *Proceedings of the Rabbinical Assembly* 32 (1968), pp. 229-240 = David Golinkin, ed., *Proceedings of the Committee on Jewish Law and Standards of the Conservative Movement 1927-1970*, vol. 2, Jerusalem, 1997, pp. 914-925.

2. Klein, Isaac, *A Guide to Jewish Religious Practice*, New York, 1992, p. 507.

3. Rank, Perry and Freeman, Gordon, eds., *Moreh Derekh: The Rabbinical Assembly Rabbi's Manual*, New York, 1998, pp. C35-C39.

4. Susskind Goldberg, Monique and Villa, Diana, *Za'akat Dalot: Halakhic Solutions for the Agunot of Our Time*, Jerusalem, 2006, chapter 1, pp. 3-100 [Hebrew with an English abstract].

5. Susskind Goldberg, Monique and Villa, Diana, "Prenuptial Agreements: A Solution for the *Agunah* Problem of Our Time", *To Learn and To Teach*, Number 4, Jerusalem, 2007.

54. Is It a Sin to Remain Single?

QUESTION

Dear Rabbi,

I am Jew. Does Judaism consider it a sin if a person does not marry? Is there any prophet who did not marry?

ANSWER

Marriage and family life are important and central institutions in Judaism. Two main reasons are given in the sources for this insistence that people marry.

1. "It is not good that man is alone"

The first reason is stated in Genesis 2:18: "And the Lord God said, 'It is not good that man is alone; I shall make him a helpmate opposite him' ". And in *Proverbs* 18:22: "Who finds a wife finds a great good, and obtains favor of the Lord".

People are not meant to be alone, as it is written in the Talmud (*Yevamot* 62b): "R. Tanḥum stated in the name of R. Ḥanilai: Any man who has no wife lives without joy, without blessing, and without goodness" (see also *Midrash Aggadah* on Genesis 2:18; *Bereshit Rabbah* (Vilna) 17:2; *Kohelet Rabbah* (Vilna) 9 and more).

This opinion is also expressed in the codes. In *Even Ha'ezer* 1:1, the Rema states: "Whoever does not have a wife lives without blessings, without Torah... and is not called a man".

To live a full and meaningful life, men and women need to find a soul mate to share the hardship and the blessings, the pain and the joy, only then can they reach the ideal state in which they were meant to be from the creation; only then can they be called human.

2. "Be fruitful and multiply"

The second reason for marriage that we find in the sources is the Biblical commandment to have children (Genesis 1:28 and elsewhere). According to Jewish law, men are commanded to marry in order to bring children into the world. This is what we read in *Even Ha'ezer* (*ibid.*): "Every man must marry a woman in order to observe the commandment to be fruitful and multiply". According to R. Joseph Karo (*ibid.* 1:3), if a man did not marry by age twenty, the *Beit Din* must force him to do so.

R. Moshe Isserles (the Rema), does not accept R. Joseph Karo's opinion. He writes (*ibid.*) that "in our time" (i.e. the 16th century) men are no longer forced by the authorities to marry for the sake of having children. The Rema even allows a man to marry a woman who cannot have children.

According to Maimonides (Laws of Marriage 15:3), if a person wants to dedicate himself to Torah learning, he does not have to be forced to marry.

In conclusion, I would say that to remain single is not a transgression, but Judaism sees family life as an ideal.

About your question concerning the prophets, the Bible usually does not speak about the prophets' family life, so it is difficult to say which prophet was married and which was not.

Rabbi Monique Susskind Goldberg
September 2007

FOR FURTHER READING

1. Dorff, Elliot, *"This is My Beloved, This is My Friend": A Rabbinic Letter on Intimate Relations*, New York, 1996.

2. Golinkin, David, in: *Responsa of the Va'ad Halakhah of the Rabbinical Assembly of Israel*, vol. 3 (5748-5749), pp. 87-88 [Hebrew].

55. Should a Jew Refuse to Attend an Intermarriage Ceremony in His/Her Family?

QUESTION

Dear Rabbi,

My cousin has just announced his engagement to a woman of another religious persuasion and my brother informed me he will not attend the wedding, at the suggestion of his rabbi. He feels that by attending the wedding he would be accepting this unholy marriage with which he does not agree. My brother and I (who are now grown adults with children of our own) both grew up in a Conservative household, as did my cousin. My brother has since become a strictly observant Orthodox Jew. I, however, feel his refusal to attend will cause my cousin and our family great pain. His view is that God and the Torah come first and family second. My feelings towards Judaism and these teachings, along with my feelings for my brother, have since become strained and I am feeling resentful. Although I had always agreed with the importance of maintaining a Jewish household, my cousin has chosen his path and I will not punish him or anyone else for doing so. My question to you is, do you agree with my brother's decision and, if so, how can you justify it? If not, what can I say to my brother to change his mind?

ANSWER

Intermarriage frequently results in assimilation. This is why the Bible, out of concern for the survival of the Israelites, already warns about its consequences by pointing out that the foreign partner "will turn your children away from Me to worship other gods" (Deuteronomy 7:4). The Sages in the Talmud warned that marriage with non-Jewish women would lead Jewish men to idolatry (*Shabbat* 17b). These men and their descendants would lose their Jewish identity. Statistics prove that in our days, children of mixed marriages are much more likely to assimilate, and they and their descendants will be lost to the Jewish people forever.

According to Jewish law, it is forbidden to marry a non-Jew. The major codes consider this to be a Biblical prohibition derived from the verse "You shall not intermarry with them: do not give your daughters to their sons or take their daughters for your sons" (Deuteronomy 7:3) and therefore forbid marital relations with non-Jews (see Maimonides, Laws of Forbidden Sexual Relations 12:1 and *Even Ha'ezer* 16:1).[6]

Jewish law prohibits supporting those who transgress the law in any way, even by means of words. For example, *Mishnah Shevi'it* 4:3 does not allow a person to give even verbal support to a Jew who does commerce with Sabbatical year produce. Since marrying a non-Jew is forbidden, if we attend the wedding, we are showing that we, in some way, accept this behavior.

Many rabbinic organizations forbid their members to be present at a mixed marriage. This is due to the fact that the presence of a figure with authority such as a rabbi at such a wedding indicates it is acceptable at some level to intermarry. Indeed, in the Conservative Movement there is a Standard of Rabbinic Practice that a rabbi who officiates in any way at an intermarriage is liable to expulsion from the Rabbinical Assembly.

If your brother decides not to attend, let us hope your cousin will understand, considering that he is, after all, following his rabbi's advice. Your brother could also choose to be at the reception as a mark of affection for your cousin and not at the ceremony. He could also go to the reception for a short time and then gracefully leave, thus making clear to the family, that as much as he appreciates his cousin, he is deeply upset about the intermarriage. He should understand that coming to the wedding does not prove in any way that he supports intermarriage.

I hope this is a good basis for a conversation with your brother. Good luck!

Rabbi Diana Villa

July 2003

6 Furthermore, a marriage with a non-Jew has no legal validity according to Jewish law (see *Mishnah Kiddushin* 3:12 = *Kiddushin* 66b and *Kiddushin* 68a-b; Maimonides, Laws of Marriage 4:14; *Even Ha'Ezer* 44:8).

DEATH

56. When Is Reburial Permitted?

QUESTION

Dear Rabbi,

I have looked at your website for a person to ask a question regarding what is to me a unique situation.

A member of my wife's family was buried yesterday in a proper ceremony. The problem that has arisen is that a family member who didn't really have any documentation as to the proper burial plot gave the funeral home a specific plot. The funeral home used that information to bury the deceased in another person's plot.

Please give me some insight as to how and what (if anything) is proper in such an instance according to Judaism. It hasn't been decided whether or not to pursue a reburial. It would be extremely helpful to have an understanding of Jewish law should a family member want to discuss reburial.

ANSWER

I am sorry for your wife's loss and for the problems with the burial.

Jewish Law in general forbids reburial. However, it permits reburial in very specific cases (*Yoreh De'ah* 363:1):

1. Reburial in the land of Israel.

2. Reburial in a family plot.

3. When there is a risk to the grave. i.e., water leaking into the grave.

4. When the deceased was put in a grave that does not belong to him and the owner does not agree to give it up (see *ibid.*, *Pithei Teshuvah*, subparag. 3).

The last case seems to describe your situation.

I hope that you can reach an agreement with the owner of the plot so that you don't have to rebury your wife's relative.

Rabbi Monique Susskind Goldberg
June 2008

FOR FURTHER READING

1. Ginzberg, Louis, *The Responsa of Prof. Louis Ginzberg*, edited by David Golinkin, New York and Jerusalem, 1996, pp. 190-198.

2. Greenwald, Yekutiel Yehudah, *Kol Bo Al Aveilut*, Jerusalem and New York, 1973, pp. 246-247 [Hebrew].

57. Is It Permissible to Prolong the Period of Mourning When Someone Dies Immediately Before a Festival?

QUESTION

Dear Rabbi,

I wanted to ask if there is anything in Conservative *responsa* written about the mourning rituals when a person dies close to a festival.

As it stands in traditional *halakhah*, if someone dies before Yom Kippur, then Yom Kippur would end the period of *shiv'ah*, and Sukkot would end the period of *shloshim*. As someone who believes that the Jewish mourning cycle is very useful psychologically, has there been any response with regards to this to allow for a longer period of mourning?

If you can point me in the direction of the specific *responsa* related to this, then I can look for the book and find it.

ANSWER

Halakhah is very specific about the mourning period for death occurring close to the holidays. *Yoreh De'ah* 399:1-3 describes the different situations when the burial occurs just before a holiday, a week before, or during the intermediary days (of Passover and Sukkot). In all those cases, the mourning time is shortened.

There is no different approach in Conservative *responsa* on this subject.

169

You are right about the psychological benefit of the Jewish mourning rituals, but from a Jewish point of view, life takes precedence. Even in a time of bereavement it is important to take part in the yearly cycle of festivals because life continues and to take part in the celebrations of the holidays also helps the bereaved to overcome his/her sorrows.

This being said, there is no impediment for you to find different ways to remember your dear one and share the memories with others, especially during the first year of mourning and on the *yahrzeit*.

Rabbi Monique Susskind Goldberg
February 2007

58. Is It Permissible to Put a Tombstone on the Grave of a Ten-Day-Old Baby?

QUESTION

Dear Rabbi,

Many years ago, a close relative who was a Conservative Jew, gave birth to a baby who lived for ten days. The baby was buried, yet the mother was led to believe that the baby was not considered hers because the traditional *brit* [circumcision] and naming were not performed. We have found the burial site and would like to put up a small stone, since currently there is nothing there to signify a burial site. Is this allowed under Jewish law?

ANSWER

According to the major codes of Jewish law, a baby who has reached full term requires all mourning rituals even if he lived only one day (Maimonides, Laws of Mourning 1:7; *Yoreh De'ah* 374:8).

However, some medieval sources rule that not only babies who were born before nine months of pregnancy, but in some cases even those who reached full term, do not require mourning rituals (the school of Rashi: see *Sefer Ha'orah*, part 2, parag. 147; *Maḥzor Vitri*, parag. 276; and *Hagahot Maimoniot* on Maimonides, *ibid*. subpar. 4).

If the baby had not reached full term and died before 30 days, the major codes agree that no rituals are required except for burial, since a baby was not considered viable until then.

A 1987 Conservative *responsum* mandates mourning rituals for a premature baby that lived at least 30 days. A 1992 Conservative *responsum* mandates the observance of all mourning rituals for all babies who passed away, even before 30 days (since babies today are considered viable before 30 days).[7] Both *responsa* are listed below.

In addition, one is required to give the baby a name at the graveside if it was not done while it was alive (see *Yoreh De'ah* 263:5 and Tukachinsky listed below). This was due to the beliefs

171

that the name ensures that the baby will receive pity from Heaven, will come to life when the dead are resurrected and will then be able to recognize his father (*Beit Yosef, Yoreh De'ah* 263, *s.v. katav ga'on* in the name of the *Rosh* and *Rabeinu Yeruḥam*).

There is an obligation to mark the place in which someone is buried by a sign or a tombstone for the following three reasons:

1. To mark the impure place (*Mo'ed Katan* 5a, Maimonides, Laws of Corpse Uncleanness 8:9).

2. To inform anyone who wants to visit and pray of the location of the site (*Responsa Yad Yitzḥak* 3:38).

3. To show respect for the soul that hovers around the burial site (*Zohar, Lekh Lekha* 83b).

Since all the reasons I noted are just as valid for a newborn baby as for an older person, it makes sense to put up a stone on the site.

Rabbi Diana Villa
July 2007

FOR FURTHER READING

1. Aizenberg, Isidoro, "Mourning for a Newborn", *Responsa 1980-1990*, New York, 2005, pp. 628-631.

2. Dickstein, Stephanie, "Jewish Ritual Practice Following the Death of an Infant Who Lives Less Than Thirty-One Days", *Responsa 1991-2000*, ed. by Kassel Abelson and David Fine, New York, 2002, pp. 439-449.

3. Greenwald, Yekutiel Yehudah, *Kol Bo al Aveilut*, New York, 1956, pp. 378-388 [Hebrew].

4. Tukachinsky, Yeḥiel Michel, *Gesher Haḥayyim*, Jerusalem, 1960, pp. 146-147, 303 [Hebrew].

---

7 Since according to some rabbinic opinions a child can enter the World to Come before 30 days, i.e., at the time of conception, birth or circumcision, this would seem to strengthen the opinion that when the soul departs s/he must be properly mourned (see *Sanhedrin* 110b, quoted by Dickstein, p. 446, note 11).

59. What Is the Proper Procedure for the *Viddui* Recited by a Dying Person?

QUESTION

Dear Rabbi,

I am a resident and family counselor in a Jewish nursing home in Delaware. When residents are dying and a rabbi is not present, I conduct a *viddui* service for them and their families. I am interested in learning more about the *viddui* said at the end of life – history, technique, family involvement, etc.

When my father died, a rabbi did a service at his bedside which was very moving. Since he was unconscious, we (his children, grandchildren and our mother) asked him for forgiveness and forgave him for anything he might have done to hurt us (please understand he was a fantastic father and person!). It was very moving, and I would like to learn more.

ANSWER

Viddui means to confess our sins before God.

Jewish law requires a person who is near death to recite a *viddui* [confession] (see *Shabbat* 32a). The *viddui* expiates one's sins (see *Mishnah Sanhedrin* 6:2 = *Sanhedrin* 43b), thus the person leaves this world with a clean slate, making him worthy of the World to Come and of Resurrection (see Maimonides, Laws of Repentance 7:1; *Yoreh De'ah* 338:1). On a psychological level, it can help the dying person to leave this world in a calmer frame of mind.

We are told in the Talmud that Rabbi Eliezer says that one should repent a day before one's death. His students asked him how this was possible as we do not know the day of our death. Rabbi Eliezer answered that this is why one should repent every day (see *Avot* 2:10 and *Shabbat* 153a). It follows that if one has not done so before, one is required to repent on his or her deathbed.

In case of a sick person, the *Shulḥan Arukh* (*Yoreh De'ah, ibid.*) explains that one should be careful not to distress the patient and to explain that saying *viddui* does not mean that death is

173

imminent. Some codifiers suggest that a patient on his deathbed should ask for forgiveness from all those against whom he has sinned (see *Hamadrikh*, p. 105).

If the person is capable of doing so, certain Psalms should be read (such as chapters 16, 23, 121) before reciting the *viddui* itself (see *Gesher Haḥayyim*, p. 34).

There are a few versions of the *viddui* in the Hebrew original and in translation; they can be shorter or longer depending on the dying person's particular situation. If a person can barely speak, he should say: "May my death be atonement for all my sins". He can also say *Ashamnu*, the *viddui* we pronounce during the Yom Kippur services, or the following brief form of confession:

> I acknowledge unto You, my God and God of my fathers, that both my cure and my death depend on Your will. May it be Your will to heal me. Yet if You have decreed that I shall die of this disease, may my death expiate all my sins, iniquities and transgressions which I have committed before You. Grant me shelter in the shadow of Your wings and a portion in the Garden of Eden, and let me merit the Resurrection and the life of bliss in the World to Come, which is reserved for the righteous (*Yoreh De'ah* 338:2).

The person can also make a mental confession if he is unable to do so verbally (*ibid.*). The rabbi or someone else present can confess for the person if he cannot do it at all for himself (because of lack of strength or consciousness).

There is also a custom to give charity at the time of the *viddui* (see *Gesher Haḥayyim*, p. 35).

Since there is leeway allowed in the wording of the confession, it is possible to add whatever is appropriate for the sick person or the family and will make the moment more meaningful to them. There is no fixed role for family members.

I hope that this answer is helpful to you as you continue to help the elderly patients in your nursing home.

Rabbi Diana Villa
April 2004

FOR FURTHER READING

1. Goldin, Hyman E., *Hamadrich: The Rabbi's Guide*, New York, 1939, p. 105.

2. Klein, Isaac, *Eit Laledet V'eit Lamut*, translated and edited by David Golinkin, Jerusalem, 1991, pp. 20-21 and note 12 [Hebrew].

3. Rank, Perry and Freeman, Gordon, eds., *The Rabbinical Assembly Rabbi's Manual*, New York, 1998, pp. D23-D26.

4. Tukachinsky, Yehiel Michel, *Gesher Hahayyim*, second edition, Jerusalem, 1960, p. 34 [Hebrew].

60. What Is the *Yizkor* Service?

QUESTION

Dear Rabbi,

What is the *Yizkor* Service? How does it differ from other services? Is one required to attend *Yizkor* services during the first year after a relative passes away?

ANSWER

A "*Yizkor* Service" or "Memorial Service" [*Hazkarat Neshamot*] for close relatives who have died is traditionally conducted at the close of the main festivals, i.e. on the last day of Passover, on Shavuot (the second day in the Diaspora), on Yom Kippur, and on Shemini Atzeret, the second holiday that falls at the end of Sukkot. During the service, each person remembers his relatives who have departed.

Usually, the memorial service comes after the reading of the Torah and the *Haftarah* (see, for example, *Orah Hayyim* 621:6 in the Rema).

The word "*Yizkor*" ["he shall remember"] is the opening word of the memorial prayer. The *Yizkor* prayer is followed by *El Malei Rahamim*, a prayer for the soul of the departed. It is also an accepted practice that the entire community recite a memorial prayer for those who were killed in the Holocaust, and for soldiers in the Israel Defense Forces who died defending the Jewish State.

During the first year after the passing of a mother or father, there is a custom not to attend the *Yizkor* service, but this is not mandatory. One of the reasons mentioned is that since the pain of such mourners is fresh, they would disturb the congregation by their crying (see *Entziklopedia Talmudit*, column 608).

Rabbi Monique Susskind Goldberg
September 2004

FOR FURTHER READING

1. *Encyclopaedia Judaica*, second edition, Jerusalem, 2007, *Hazkarat Neshamot*, vol. 8, pp. 496-497.

2. *Entziklopedia Talmudit*, vol. 8, Jerusalem, 1957, *Hazkarat Neshamot*, columns 603-609 [Hebrew].

3. Golinkin, David, *Responsa of the Va'ad Halakhah of the Rabbinical Assembly of Israel* 2 (5747), p. 24 and note 3 [Hebrew].

4. Tukachinsky, Yeḥiel Michel, *Gesher Haḥayyim*, second edition, Jerusalem, 1960, pp. 335-340 [Hebrew].

RITUAL

61. Are Joint *Aliyot* Permissible?

QUESTION

Dear Rabbi,

According to Jewish law, is there a prohibition of calling up more than one person at a time for an *aliyah*? I'm trying to trace the history and range of opinions on "group *aliyot*".

Many thanks in advance for your time and consideration.

ANSWER

There are three different possibilities that could be taken into account if we want to call two people up for an *aliyah*: both of them could read the Torah together, both of them could pronounce the blessings together, or one could say the blessing before the reading and one after it.

1. Reading the Torah Portion Together:

In *Tannaitic* times, every person who was called up to the Torah, read his own portion (see *Mishnah Megillah* 4:1 = *Megillah* 21a).

According to the sources, only one person could read Torah at a time. The reason given is that when the words are pronounced by two people at the same time, people cannot hear the words properly (see *Tosefta Megillah* 3:20, ed. Lieberman, p. 359; *Megillah*. 21b; Rashi *ad loc.*, s.v. *ubilvad*; *Rosh Hashanah* 27a; Jerusalem Talmud, *Berakhot* 5:3, 9c and *Megillah* 4:1, 74d).

In the Middle Ages, people lost the ability to read Torah themselves; therefore, there is usually a Torah reader who does so. The person who goes up to the Torah only says the blessings and follows the reader's reading. A person who has the expertise necessary to read may do so in addition to the blessings, but according to *halakhah*, two people cannot read together, even the person called up to the Torah together with the Torah reader (see *Oraḥ Ḥayyim* 141:2).

2. Saying the Blessings Together:

In *Tannaitic* times, not every reader recited the blessings before and after his reading like today. One blessing was recited by the first reader before the entire reading, and one blessing was recited by the last reader after the completion of the entire reading (see *Mishnah Megillah* 4:1.).

But in the first generation of Babylonian *Amora'im* (Rav and Samuel), an enactment was already established that every person going up to the Torah said a blessing before and after he read his portion. The reason for this change was to avoid the possibility that people coming in late or leaving early would mistakenly believe that the Torah could be read without a blessing before or after the reading (*Megillah* 21b).

According to Rabbi Zeira (third generation Israeli *Amora*), the reason for the rule that two people cannot read the Torah together is "on account of the blessing" (Jerusalem Talmud, *Megillah* 4:1, 74d).

Since Rabbi Zeira does not explain his dictum, it is not clear if he meant that two people pronouncing the blessing together cannot be heard properly, or that there is a problem related to the blessing itself.

Two halakhic authorities, the Ribash and the *Magen Avraham*, based themselves on Rabbi Zeira to express their objections to two people saying the blessings together either before and after the Torah reading, or before and after the *Haftarah* reading.

The Ribash expressed his disapproval of two people reading together from the Prophets (the *Haftarah*), since this would entail one person reciting the blessings in vain (see *Responsa Ribash*, No. 36). The *Magen Avraham* was opposed to joint *aliyot* on the basis of Rabbi Zeira, but he admitted that this ruling was contradicted by the common practice on *Simhat Torah* (see *Magen Avraham* to *Orah Hayyim* 669).

A blessing that is unnecessary [*berakhah she'einah tzerikhah*] is considered a blessing in vain [*berakhah levatalah*] and cannot be pronounced according to Jewish law. It entails pronouncing God's name in vain (see Maimonides, Laws of Blessings 11:16; *Orah Hayyim* 215:4).

Several people are allowed to recite a blessing at the same time, when they all have the obligation to pronounce the blessing (as in the blessing of the *tzizit* – see *Orah Hayyim* 8:5). However, when several people do one *mitzvah* together like putting up a *mezuzah*, one says the blessing for all of them. It is redundant for two people to pronounce the blessing for the same *mitzvah* (see *Tosefta Berakhot* 6:15, ed. Lieberman, p. 37 and his commentary in *Tosefta Kifshutah*, p. 117).

Torah reading is a **communal** and not an **individual** obligation; the blessings that are attached to it are a way of honoring the Torah when it is read in public (*Oraḥ Ḥayyim* 139:8, based on *Megillah* 23a). Therefore, **if two people pronounce the blessings together for the same reading, it is redundant, and in vain**. Thus, this is not an option when two people are called up to the Torah together.

3. Having a different person pronounce the blessing before and after an *aliyah*:

As we saw, according to the original *Tannaitic* custom, where there was only one blessing at the beginning and another one at the end, it was not a problem that one person recited the blessing before the reading and another person recited the blessing after the reading. Since the Torah reading is a communal and not an individual obligation, the purpose of the blessings is to give honor to the Torah in public and it does not really matter who says these blessings (see Reisner, p. 28 and Golinkin, pp. 93-96). Thus, two people could come up for each *aliyah* and one would recite the blessing before the reading and one would recite the blessing after the reading.

This solution seems to be the most acceptable way for two people to have a joint *aliyah*.

Finally, extra people can be called to the Torah on Shabbat. This is a simple way to honor more people without resorting to joint *aliyot* (*Mishnah Megillah* 4:2; *Oraḥ Ḥayyim* 282:1).

Rabbi Diana Villa
September 2006

FOR FURTHER READING

1. Abelson, Kassel, *"Aliyot* for Couples", *Responsa 1991-2000*, New York, 2002, pp. 36-42.

2. Golinkin, David, *The Status of Women in Jewish Law: Responsa*, Jerusalem, 2001, pp. 93-96 [Hebrew].

3. Reisner, Avram Israel, *"Joint Aliyot"*, *Responsa 1991-2000*, New York, 2002, pp. 21-35.

62. May a Child Holding a *Ḥumash* Count as the Tenth Person in a *Minyan*?

QUESTION

Dear Rabbi,

How would you respond to options for attaining a *minyan* when only nine people are present, e.g., nine and a boy holding a *ḥumash*? Many people here feel that if there is a mourner present he/she should not be sent away if they have the possibility of reciting *Kaddish*.

ANSWER

Kaddish is considered one of the "sanctified things" [*devarim shebekedushah*] that may only be recited in a quorum of ten adults, a *minyan* (see *Mishnah Megillah* 4:3; *Oraḥ Ḥayyim* 55:1).

R. Joseph Karo, in *Shulḥan Arukh, ibid*. 55:4, mentions the custom of saying sanctified things in a quorum of only nine people and a child older than six years old who understands to whom the prayers are directed. However, he personally is against this practice.

In his gloss on the same paragraph, the Rema mentions the custom of adding as a tenth person a child holding a *Ḥumash* in his hand. This custom is based on a passage in the Babylonian Talmud, *Berakhot* 47b saying that a child can be counted among the ten for the grace after the meal and on the commentary of *Tosafot ad loc.* (*Berakhot* 48a, *s.v. velet*). The Rema does not accept the practice of saying sanctified things in a quorum of nine adults and a child. He adds, however, that some authorities accept the practice in case of an emergency [*she'at hadeḥak*].

In conclusion, I think you have a basis to allow the mourner to recite *kaddish* even if you have only nine adults and a child (six years old or more) because it could be described as "an emergency". I would not use this as a regular practice each time you are lacking a quorum of ten.

Rabbi Monique Susskind Goldberg
February 2006

63. May I Pray Barefoot?

QUESTION

Dear Rabbi,

I know this is a little odd, but I really feel more "grounded" when *davening* barefoot. I am aware that – at least in Orthodox circles – this is frowned upon, since one has to be fully dressed, as if facing a dignitary, when engaging in prayer. I usually *daven* while wearing shoes, just to be on the safe side! But for me, *davening* barefoot is in no way intended as disrespect. In fact, it increases my *kavanah* [concentration]. Is such a "spiritual-emotional" reason a valid reason on which to make such a decision? Is this a matter of personal choice and conscience or is there an appropriate Conservative answer to this? Is it worse to daven barefoot during *Shaharit* [morning service] when I wear a *tallit* [prayer shawl] and *tefillin* [phylacteries] rather than during *Minhah* [afternoon service] and *Ma'ariv* [evening service], due to supposed "dishonor" to these ritual objects?

ANSWER

Public worship requires certain standards. Someone who is a *poheah* cannot serve as *shaliah tzibbur* [prayer leader] or read from the Torah or bless the people if he is a *kohen* (*Mishnah Megillah* 4:6 = *Megillah* 24a). Rashi (*ad loc.*) quotes the tractate *Soferim* (14:12, ed. Higger, p. 265) and explains that this is considered indecent exposure. Maimonides (Laws of Prayer and of the Priestly Blessing 8:12) explains that the shoulders must be covered, and Rabbi Yosef Karo (*Orah Hayyim* 53:13) says that a *poheah* i.e., someone with torn clothes or uncovered arms, may not serve as a prayer leader. The person fulfilling these ritual functions must respect the congregation he is leading. However, even in such attire, certain public functions such as leading the responsive reading of the *Shema* (which was done from one's own seat, therefore no one can see how one is dressed) and translating the Biblical reading (which was not considered such an important function), as well as praying as an individual in the synagogue, were allowed.

In the following folio (*Megillah* 24b), the rabbis discuss whether these norms apply to minors and adults and conclude affirmatively for both, since it is a question of respect for the congregation.

It is indecent and disrespectful to lead the congregation for certain parts of the service (whether it be for *Shaharit, Minhah* or *Ma'ariv*) while parts of the body are exposed. Although the rabbis do not explicitly include being barefoot as a sign of disrespect, it is not accepted decorum in the synagogue.

For at least 1,800 years the rabbis have held that there is a proper dress code for public worship, insofar as those who lead services. They set the example for the rest of the congregation. Decorum is important during services.

In 1990, the Law Committee of the Rabbinical Assembly of Israel unanimously approved a *responsum* that stresses:

> In the synagogue we must be much more scrupulous about modesty. We must honor the place and the occasion. The guiding principle must be to view the synagogue as a "small sanctuary" and prayer, as the standing of man before God. And thus, we must dress in the synagogue as we would dress to go greet a VIP – in dignified and modest clothing (see the *responsum* by Rabbi Chaim Wiener).

Since the sources cited above discuss public worship, one can be more lenient in private worship. The only limitation is not to show private parts [*ervah*] (see *Berakhot* 24b-25a; Maimonides, Laws of the Reading of the *Shema* 3:17; *Orah Hayyim* 74:1). Therefore, if you pray at home, without a *minyan*, it might not be considered as disrespectful to pray barefoot as it perhaps would be in a synagogue or with a prayer quorum.

Rabbi Diana Villa
March 2005

FOR FURTHER READING

Wiener, Chaim, "Women and the Wearing of Pants" in: *Responsa of the Va'ad Halakhah of the Rabbinical Assembly of Israel*, vol. 4 (5750-5752), pp. 53-64 [Hebrew with an English summary; also available at http://www.responsafortoday.com].

64. May a Weekday Torah Reading Be Postponed until *Minḥah?*

QUESTION

Dear Rabbi,

Is the reading of the Torah on Mondays and Thursdays limited to the *Shaḥarit* service?

If it is only possible to obtain a *minyan* in the afternoon, may the Torah reading be postponed until *Minḥah?*

ANSWER

The *Mishnah* (*Megillah* 4:1) says that the Torah must be read on Monday and Thursday, Shabbat afternoon, Rosh Ḥodesh, Holidays and Shabbat morning. The Talmud (*Bava Kamma* 82a) ascribes the first three readings to Ezra the Scribe. Maimonides ascribes the Torah readings on Shabbat, Monday and Thursday **mornings** to Moses our Teacher. He ascribes only the Shabbat afternoon reading to Ezra the Scribe (see Laws of Prayer and of the Priestly Blessing 12:1).

Rabbi Joseph Karo, in his commentary on Maimonides, explains that only some versions of the *Mishneh Torah* [Maimonides' code of law] include the word *beshaḥarit* (in the morning, at the morning service; see *Kesef Mishneh, ad loc.*). If so, one might claim that the Torah reading can take place all day long.[8]

Rabbi Joseph Karo rules in *Oraḥ Ḥayyim* 135:1 that the Torah must be read on Monday, Thursday and Shabbat afternoon, and the *Mishnah Berurah* (*ad loc.*, subparag. 1) explains that *bedi'avad* [after the fact, if it wasn't done in the morning for some reason] the Torah can be read at any time of the day.

Rabbi Judah ben Israel Aszod describes the case of three rabbis returning from a rabbinic convention who prayed at a hotel in the morning, but didn't read Torah. Upon arriving at a

---

8 There is a rule that laws that may be observed during the whole day may be observed anytime during the day (*Mishnah Megillah* 2:6 = *Megillah* 20b). However, people should perform them as early as possible, to avoid the possibility of forgetting to do them entirely.

village in the late afternoon, they were able to gather a *minyan* and read Torah at the local synagogue (see *Responsa Yehudah Ya'aleh*, part 1, *Oraḥ Ḥayyim*, No. 51).

As you can see, there is precedent for reading Torah in the afternoon; however this should be done only when the reading could not take place in the morning. It is a well-known principle that *zerizim makdimin lemitzvot* [the zealous do their religious duty as early as possible] (see *Pesaḥim* 4a); an example is performing circumcision on the morning of the eighth day even though it could take place all day (see *Yoreh De'ah* 268:1).

We also wish to ensure that postponing the reading does not lead to not doing it altogether if it becomes very late. For these reasons, Torah reading in the afternoon should not be done *a priori*, but only as a last resort.

Rabbi Diana Villa
June 2007

FOR FURTHER READING

Golinkin, David, "The Timing of *Hakafot* on *Simḥat Torah*", in: *Responsa of the Va'ad Halakhah of the Rabbinical Assembly of Israel*, vol. 2 (5747), pp. 23-24, [Hebrew with English summary; also available at http://www.responsafortoday.com].

65. How Should We Proceed If the Wrong Torah Was Taken Out of the Ark?

QUESTION

Dear Rabbi,

I would like to ask your opinion about a situation that happened in my synagogue. This morning at the *minyan*, a Torah Scroll was taken out of the Ark. When it was opened, the reader saw that it was not the scroll that had been rolled to the reading of the day. The rabbi was asked whether to replace it with the scroll already set at the proper reading or to roll the scroll that had been taken out and read from it. His decision went counter to what I would have selected intuitively. Later in a quiet setting, when asked to actually look up the procedure in the *Shulḥan Arukh* or another source, he most arrogantly refused, belittling the right of people to question what he does. While acknowledging his authority to decide, but rejecting his notion of papal infallibility, I would still like to know what the proper procedure should be according to the sources.

ANSWER

I am sorry about the attitude of the rabbi who missed a good opportunity to teach the laws concerning the Torah reading. Here are my conclusions about this question:

1. On the one hand, the sources clearly state that one should not roll a Torah scroll in public "because of the honor of the congregation" – *kevod hatzibbur*. It would not be respectful to oblige the congregation to wait for the scroll to be rolled to the right place (see Maimonides, Laws of Prayer and of the Priestly Blessing 12:23; *Oraḥ Ḥayyim* 144:3).

The authorities rely upon a passage in the *Mishnah* which describes the *Yom Kippur* service during the Temple period (*Mishnah Sotah* 7:7 = *Sotah* 40b). The High Priest would read from a Torah scroll a passage from Leviticus, close the Torah, and then recite a second passage from the book of Numbers by heart so as not to have to roll the scroll in public while the public was waiting.

This is why when it is necessary to read a passage from the Torah in addition to the regular reading, the new passage should be read from a second scroll so as to avoid rolling the scroll in public (Maimonides *ibid.*; *Tur Oraḥ Ḥayyim* 144).

However if there is only one *Sefer Torah* available, the public "renounces its honor" in order to fulfill its obligation (*Oraḥ Ḥayyim ibid.*, *Mishnah Berurah*, subparag. 16 and *Magen Avraham*, subparag. 7).

2. On the other hand, the Talmudic passage on the *Mishnah* quoted above (*Sotah* 41a) states that the reason the High Priest did not read the second passage from another scroll is that if he did so, the public might have thought that the scroll which he had before him was *pagum* [defective]. This explanation was codified by Maimonides (Laws of the Service of the Day of the Atonement 3:10; cf. a similar ruling in *Oraḥ Ḥayyim* 144:4).

From this example and others, one can conclude that the "honor of the Torah" is more important that the "honor of the public". The public can choose to relinquish its honor, as in the situation when there is only one Torah scroll. This is why, according to some authorities, in a case where the wrong Torah scroll was already taken out of the Ark, one should roll the Torah to the proper place so as not to make it appear that this scroll is defective (see *Yalkut Yosef*).

3. Another argument to justify the decision of reading from the Torah scroll which was already taken out is the principle that one should not "pass over a commandment" [*ein ma'avirim al hamitzvot*] (see *Yalkut Yosef*). When one touches an object with the intention of doing a *mitzvah* with it, one cannot stop this action and do a *mitzvah* involving another object. For example, if one put *tefillin* in the same bag as the *tallit*, it should not be put above the *tallit*, to make sure that one does not touch the *tefillin* first, because if one does touch the *tefillin* first, one must put the *tefillin* on before the *tallit* (*Oraḥ Ḥayyim* 25:1; see other examples in *Megillah* 6b, or *Magen Avraham* on *Oraḥ Ḥayyim* 274:1, which addresses the issue of how to deal with the two *ḥallot* on Shabbat in order not to ignore one of them).

In our case, since the scroll was already taken out of the Ark, one must read from it and not read from another one.

In conclusion, the "honor of the public" is a very important consideration and whenever possible, a Torah scroll should not be rolled while the congregation is sitting and waiting. However, in circumstances as the one you describe, the public should forfeit its honor for the sake of the "honor of the Torah", and also because "one should not pass over a commandment".

Rabbi Monique Susskind Goldberg
August 2004

FOR FURTHER READING

Yosef, Yitzḥak, *Yalkut Yosef*, vol. 2, Jerusalem, 1990, to *Oraḥ Ḥayyim* 144, parag. 2, pp. 168-169 [Hebrew].

66. What Is the Correct Blessing on Chocolate-Covered Raisins?

QUESTION

Shalom,

A vending machine was recently installed in an Orthodox institution selling chocolate-covered raisins. The question arose as to what blessing must be pronounced before eating them. There are different halakhic opinions on which blessing must be pronounced, whether it is over the raisins or over the chocolate. Since people may be confused as to how to proceed, the institution decided that the chocolate-covered raisins should be removed from the machine.

Rather than avoid a decision, which approach would you take? Since there is a general blessing that can be said when in doubt, may we pronounce it even though this would appear valid only *bedi'avad* (after the fact)? What would be a reasonable way to, on the one hand take *halakhah* seriously, but on the other hand, not let it paralyze us because of an attempt to satisfy all opinions?

ANSWER

Jewish law rules that when two foods are eaten together, we must decide which one of them is the *ikar* or primary food and which one is the *tafel* or secondary food and bless according to the primary food (if one of the foods is from the five grains, that blessing supersedes all others and the rule does not apply).

The issue of what is the *ikar* and what is the *tafel* in the chocolate-covered raisins varies according to individual preference (*Oraḥ Ḥayyim* 212:1).

There are different halakhic opinions as to what blessing should be pronounced for chocolate-covered raisins. If the raisins are the main food, the blessing for fruit (*bore pri ha'etz*) should be recited. If the chocolate is the main food, the blessing said for foods that are not fruit, vegetables or products from the five grains (*shehakol nihya bidvaro*) should be said. There is even an opinion that two different blessings must be pronounced because

194

one intends to eat both foods equally (Rabbi Moshe Feinstein, *Igrot Moshe, Orah Hayyim*, part 3, No. 31).

In any case, it is quite obvious that the solution is not to remove the chocolate-covered raisins from the machine. While there is a disagreement as to what the correct blessing is, there could either be a note on the machine saying which blessing should be recited or a note explaining the three options (depending on the eater's preference): to bless on the raisins, on the chocolate or on both. In all cases, the blessing would be *lekhathilah* (saying a blessing you consider correct in the first place) and not *bedi'avad* (after the fact).

The best path may be to bless *shehakol* for the chocolate-covered raisins, since according to some decisors saying *"shehakol"* when one is in doubt about the correct blessing is correct not only *bedi'avad* but also *lekhathilah* (see *Beit Yosef, Orah Hayyim* 204, based on *Hagahot Maimoniot* on Maimonides, Laws of Blessings, 8:10, subparag. 70, which in turn is based on *Tosafot* on *Berakhot* 40b, *s.v. Rabbi Yohanan*).

Sincerely,

Rabbi Diana Villa
September 2003

FOR FURTHER READING

Yosef, Yitzhak, *Yalkut Yosef*, part 3, Jerusalem, 1991, pp. 430-431.

SHABBAT AND HOLIDAYS

SHABBAT

67. May I Attend an Acoustic Guitar Concert on Shabbat?

QUESTION

Dear Rabbi,

Is it a violation of *halakhah* to attend a concert of acoustic guitar on Shabbat? Either way, could you provide sources which support your opinion?

ANSWER

The answer to your question is not simple and depends on a few circumstances.

1. If the player is Jewish, by playing the guitar on Shabbat, he himself is transgressing a Rabbinic decree.

   a. The Rabbis have forbidden playing instruments on Shabbat and Holidays to avoid a situation where the player would fix his instrument on Shabbat, which would be a biblical transgression (see *Beitzah* 36b; Maimonides, Laws of the Sabbath 23:4). By playing on Shabbat, the musician is thereby transgressing a Rabbinic decree. It should be added on this point that a person playing a guitar nearly always does some kind of "fixing" by tuning the guitar and stretching the strings or even replacing a broken string (see *Arukh Hashulḥan, Oraḥ Ḥayyim* 338:5). By doing so, he transgress both Biblical and Rabbinic prohibitions.

   b. According to *halakhah*, it is forbidden for a Jew to benefit from another Jew's transgression. The example given in the *Shulḥan Arukh* (*Oraḥ Ḥayyim* 318:1) is that a Jew is forbidden to eat the food cooked on Shabbat by another Jew.

2. If the player is not Jewish, there is no transgression of the Shabbat on your part, on condition that the player is playing essentially for himself or for a non-Jewish audience, and not adding special music for you.

199

A similar case is discussed in the *Shulḥan Arukh* (*Oraḥ Ḥayyim* 276:1); the question there is whether a Jew can use the light of a candle lit by a non-Jew on Shabbat. The answer is that if the non-Jew lit the candle for himself, a Jew may use it, because in the words of the Talmud "A candle for one is the same as a candle for a hundred" (*Shabbat* 122a). In other words, the light of a candle can be used by one person or by one hundred people. However, if most or even half of the people who use the light of that candle are Jewish, those Jews are committing a transgression because it looks as if the candle was lit for them (*Oraḥ Ḥayyim* 276:2). The same can be said about your concert; if most of the people in the audience are non-Jews, then, strictly speaking, you do not violate *halakhah* when you listen to a non-Jew playing the acoustic guitar on Shabbat.

However, attending an acoustic guitar concert is not really consonant with the spirit of Shabbat. The Jerusalem Talmud explains some of the decrees of the Rabbis forbidding certain activities on Shabbat (*shevut*) simply with the words "those are activities we do on weekdays" (see Jerusalem Talmud, *Eruvin* 10:13, 26d). In the same way, in our opinion going to a guitar concert is an activity for weekdays and not for Shabbat.

Rabbi Monique Susskind Goldberg
May 2007

FOR FURTHER READING

1. Bandel, Ehud, "Playing Music on Shabbat", *Et La'asot* 2 (1990), pp. 41-53 [Hebrew].

2. Golinkin, David, *An Index of Conservative Responsa and Practical Halakhic Studies: 1917-1990*, New York, 1992, pp. 61-62.

3. Golinkin, David, editor, *Proceedings of the Committee on Jewish Law and Standards of the Conservative Movement 1927-1970*, Vol. 3, Jerusalem, 1997, pp. 1314-1335.

68. May I Drive on Shabbat for the Sake of *Shlom Bayit*?

QUESTION

Shalom Rabbis,

Here is my situation. I consider myself *conservadox*, although I attend an Orthodox synagogue. My wife and I met eight years ago; she converted in the Reform Movement. After we got in contact with a *keruv* rabbi, we became more observant, and my wife converted again with an Orthodox Rabbinic court. I keep Shabbat and *kashrut*.

My wife and I have been having a difference of opinion for some time over observance. She feels that I pushed her to observe the Shabbat laws, and that now she wants to drive at times on Shabbat to do non-work or non-money-related activities (going to a park, to a birthday party, etc.). I recognize that I need to respect her decision to live how she wants to live. But she wants me to go with her on these outings, since Shabbat is the ultimate family day. Also, no one else in my family keeps Shabbat and this creates pressures.

I am very torn about what to do. Halakhicaly, I know that I shouldn't drive. But I wonder whether my wife and I went too fast, and whether it is time to take a step back so that I can meet her and so that we can then start growing together.

Do you have any ideas about this? While driving would be a transgression, is it permissible when doing so may bring *shlom bayit* (peace in the home, family harmony), if I feel that the best move for my family would be to drive once in a while?

Thank you very much.

Kol tuv.

ANSWER

I am sorry that you find yourself in such a difficult situation, and I can only try to make things clearer for you.

As you wrote, halakhicaly speaking, it is forbidden to drive on Shabbat. A person who drives on Shabbat transgresses Biblical and Rabbinic prohibitions (see below, No. 73).

Only for the sake of saving a life can one transgress a Biblical prohibition (see *Yoma* 85a-b; *Shabbat* 132a; *Orah Hayyim* 329:1).

On the other hand, *shlom bayit* is an extremely important value in Judaism. A *midrash* on Genesis 18:12-13 tells us that even God Himself lied to Avraham for the sake of preserving peace between him and Sarah (*Yevamot* 65b). So I agree that you should do everything to preserve the peace between you and your wife.

My suggestion is to try to encourage your wife to have a different approach to Shabbat. Instead of stressing what is forbidden, try to do enjoyable things together on Shabbat. It can be a time to invite friends and family for meals instead of going to them. You could take beautiful walks in your vicinity, enjoy quite reading and conversation. If you live outside of Israel, family activities, which involve outings with a car, could be done on Sundays.

Maybe your wife is not ready yet to take upon herself all the observance of Shabbat and you should let her follow her own pace, but *shlom bayit* goes in both directions and your needs and beliefs are as important as your wife's. Therefore, there must be a way to make her understand your desire to keep Shabbat, and for the sake of *shlom bayit*, she should be open to the fact that you cannot follow her in doing things against your beliefs.

I know that I did not make things easier for you, and I do hope that you will find a way to accommodate your needs as well as those of your wife. Maybe you need the advice of a counselor (a rabbi or another) who could try to help both of you find a suitable solution.

Shanah Tovah to you and to your wife,

Rabbi Monique Susskind Goldberg
October 2003

69. May I Make a Snowman on Shabbat?

QUESTION

Dear Rabbis,

Is it permissible to construct a snowman on Shabbat?

ANSWER

According to Jewish Law, you should not build anything on Shabbat, since building is one of the 39 types of labor forbidden on Shabbat (see *Shabbat* 73a; Maimonides, Laws of the Sabbath 7:1).

Maimonides ruled that bringing together different components to form a single entity is forbidden on Shabbat due to the resemblance to *Boneh* [building] (*ibid* 7:6). This includes making cheese (see *Shabbat* 95a; Maimonides *ibid*. 10:13).

Making snowballs or snowmen resembles making cheese and is therefore forbidden on Shabbat because it is considered building (see Neuwirth, p. 190).

One could argue that a snowman is a temporary building and therefore it should be allowed. But building a temporary building on Shabbat is only permitted on condition that it be destroyed on Shabbat (see *Shulḥan Arukh Harav, Oraḥ Ḥayyim* 313:21). However, in our case, the snowman is meant to last as long as possible and the length of its existence depends on the weather.

In conclusion, one should not build a snowman on Shabbat.

Rabbi Monique Susskind Goldberg
January 2009

FOR FURTHER READING

Neuwirth, Yehoshua, *Shemirat Shabbat Ke'hilkhata*, second edition, vol. 1, Jerusalem, 1989, chapter 16, parag. 42, p. 190 [Hebrew].

70. How Early May One Start Shabbat or Holidays?

QUESTION

Dear Rabbi,

How early may we start Shabbat or holidays? [The Jewish Sabbath and holidays begin before sunset on the previous evening. In the summer in particular, when it gets dark very late, many congregations decide to start earlier than required to avoid having prayers and the evening meal at a very late hour, particularly for the sake of the children].

ANSWER

The Jewish day begins on the previous evening, as our Sages teach:

> He learns [that the day begins on the previous evening] from the account of the creation of the world, where it is written, "And there was evening and there was morning, one day" (Genesis 1:5) (*Berakhot* 2a).

Therefore, Shabbat begins on Friday night when the stars come out.

The period of twilight, between sunset and nighttime, is called *bein hashmashot* (see *Mishnah Berurah* on *Oraḥ Ḥayyim* 260:2, subparag. 9).

It is not clear whether *bein hashmashot* should be considered day or night. Therefore, following the principle that when in doubt concerning a Biblical law, i.e. observing Shabbat, we follow the stricter approach [*s'feika de-Oraita leḥumra*] (*Beitzah* 3b), we must consider this period part of Shabbat (this applies to both Friday and Saturday evenings, see *Oraḥ Ḥayyim* 261:1). Thus, Shabbat begins at sunset and ends with the appearance of three stars.

Furthermore, the Talmud teaches us that we must "add from the profane to the holy" (see *Rosh Hashanah* 9a).

We must, therefore, add some time to Shabbat beyond twilight (see *Mishnah Berurah* on *Oraḥ Ḥayyim* 261:2, subpar. 19). This extra time is a minimum of 18 minutes before sunset.

However, what is the earliest time that can be considered evening and thus permissible to start observing Shabbat?

We may learn this on the basis of the time when the evening prayer may be said.

In *Mishnah Berakhot* 4:1, there are two opinions about the latest time of the afternoon prayer [*Minḥah*]. According to the Sages, the afternoon prayer may be said until dark, but, according to Rabbi Judah, only until *plag haminḥah*, an hour and a quarter before sunset.[9] This is according to the view that the prayers are said in place of the daily sacrifices (see *Berakhot* 26b). According to the Sages, the afternoon sacrifice could be offered until dark, but according to Rabbi Judah, *plag haminḥah* was the latest time to offer the afternoon sacrifice in Temple times. The Talmud concludes that both options are valid.

Once the time for reciting *Minḥah* has elapsed, the evening prayers can be said: with the advent of darkness, according to the Sages, and from *plag haminḥah* on, according to Rabbi Judah. Accordingly, Rabbi Joseph Karo and the Rema rule that one can accept Shabbat, light candles and say the evening prayer as early as *plag haminḥah* (*Oraḥ Ḥayyim* 267:2 and the Rema on 261:2).

This is valid for any Shabbat or holiday except for the first night of Shavuot, because there is a requirement according to Jewish law to count a full seven weeks between Passover and Shavuot, and the holiday may not begin until after the stars are out (see *Mishnah Berurah* on *Oraḥ Ḥayyim* 494:1, subparag. 1).

Sincerely,

Rabbi Diana Villa

July 2005

FOR FURTHER READING

Klein, Isaac, *A Guide to Jewish Religious Practice*, New York, 1992, pp. 57-58.

---

9   The hour spoken about is a proportional hour, a *sha'ah zemanit*, which is one twelfth of the daytime period between sunrise and sunset and is usually shorter or longer than the standard sixty-minute hour, according to the time of year.

71. How Should I Deal with Shabbat and Work Conflicts?

QUESTION

Dear Rabbi,

I have a dilemma, and I thought perhaps there might be a "thinking out of the box" solution, though I am doubtful. I became observant about ten years ago, and my wife and I are modern Orthodox. Most of my rabbis are *Chabadniks*, who, in this situation, are not very helpful.

I work as a building superintendent in California for a developer, and have done this for many years. The building industry in California has been extremely hectic over the past few years, and recently, many building departments have not been able to keep up with the daily volume of building inspections. As a result, some inspections have started taking place on Saturdays, and the superintendent is required to be on site for the inspector in order for the inspections to happen.

Though I have not worked a Shabbat in many years, and my employers in the past have never required me to do so (especially because of my Jewishness), that seems to have now changed. A couple of months ago I was fired from my last job for refusing to work on Shabbat. While I could probably sue over this, the result would probably be my getting blackballed in this industry.

I have now found a new job, but fear the possibility of the same problem. There is no way I am going to bring up working on Saturdays, because then I may not be considered a "team player", which is life and death in this industry. Changing professions is not a solution. I am gradually working my way into a more administrative position that will not require Saturday work, but that is a 1-3 year process. What in the world am I supposed to do? Live in the street? Do I just repent every Yom Kippur, or do I face working Monday thru Friday, not showing up on Saturday and getting fired, then start looking for work again on Monday? There must be some solution to this halakhically, but I don't know what it is.

Should I spend the night in the construction trailer Friday evenings, get my inspections done on Saturday, drive home, light

206

my candles, then say "for me, it is now Shabbat" and call the problem solved? I don't know what to do. My interaction on Saturdays would involve walking through houses with a building inspector in order for him to determine whether or not the work is complete. I don't do anything except stand there with him. I'd appreciate your thoughts.

ANSWER

I very much empathize with your problem.

As I understand it, quitting your job is not an option. The other option you suggest, starting Shabbat on Saturday or declaring Sunday Shabbat is not a solution either – you cannot change the time or day when Shabbat is observed.

The only thing I can suggest is to try to keep Shabbat and its spirit as much as possible. I suppose the inspection will not be every Shabbat. When it does fall on Shabbat, you should have a nice Shabbat celebration with your wife on Friday night (going to synagogue and have a festive Shabbat meal). On Shabbat, try to recite Shaharit before you go for your inspection. If the building site is in walking distance, avoid driving to it. If you need to travel there, use public transportation (see below, No. 73). As you are just supposed to walk around with the inspector, try to avoid writing if it is not absolutely necessary. As soon as the inspection is finished, you can join your wife and enjoy the rest of Shabbat. My other suggestion is to try to find a Rabbi who will listen to your problem with understanding and advise you about how to handle the situation.

Maybe after a while in your new company, you will be able to raise the issue of not working on Shabbat. I do hope that very soon you will be able to attain a position that allows you to have a decent income, and also allows you to live according to your faith and beliefs.

All the best,
Rabbi Monique Susskind Goldberg
February 2004

72. Is Dancing on Shabbat Allowed?

QUESTION

Dear Rabbi,

We were recently at a *Bar Mitzvah* and I noticed one of my relatives refused to dance the *horah* due to the Talmudic prohibition of dancing on Shabbat (lest music begin and a musician be tempted to repair his instrument). What is the Masorti/Conservative Movement's position on dancing on Shabbat?

ANSWER

The Rabbis forbid clapping hands and dancing on Shabbat and on the Holidays (*Mishnah Beitzah* 5:2). The Talmud (*Beitzah* 36b) explains that this enactment was decreed by the Rabbis in order to avoid the possibility of someone repairing or even building an instrument to accompany the dancing which would amount to work [*melakhah*] forbidden on Shabbat and Holidays. However, this decree was in question from the start.

Already in the Talmud there is testimony that even though it was forbidden, people did clap their hands and dance on Shabbat and the Rabbis let them, arguing that "it is better for the people to do a transgression unintentionally than to do it knowingly" (see *ibid.* 30a). In other words, people are so used to clapping hands and dancing to express their joy on Shabbat and holidays, that it would not help if the Rabbis forbade it. This is why they prefer not to say anything and not to reach a situation in which people would transgress a Rabbinic decree knowingly.

This prohibition has been the subject of dispute among authorities. Rashi, the medieval commentator, agrees with the conclusion of the Talmud that it is forbidden to dance on Shabbat to avoid the possibility of someone fixing instruments to accompany the dance (see Rashi *ibid.* 36b, *s.v. ein merakdin*). However, *Tosafot*, another medieval commentary, wanting to explain the leniency of the Rabbis as described in the Talmud (*ibid.* 30a), states that by their time (the medieval period), people were no longer adept at making instruments, so there was no longer any reason for the prohibition on dancing on Shabbat and holidays (see *Tosafot* on *Beitzah* 30a, *s.v. tnan ein metaphin*).

The same dispute is reflected in the *Shulḥan Arukh* (*Oraḥ Ḥayyim* 339:3). The author, R. Joseph Karo, forbids dancing on Shabbat and holidays but, in his gloss, the Rema presents the Ashkenazic custom which allows dancing. He justifies it as in the Talmud "better to do a transgression unintentionally..." and he also adds that some authorities allow dancing on Shabbat for the reason given by the Tosafot: people no longer know how to fix instruments.

In modern times, we still find both opinions among the authorities.

Rabbi Yeḥiel Michel Epstein, in his *Arukh Hashulḥan* (*Oraḥ Ḥayyim* 339:7), endorses the opinion of the Rema. However, it is hard for him to accept the argument of the Tosafot, as it is clear that every player knows how to change a string and how to stretch it. Therefore, on the matter of dancing, he adds that in our time there is not necessarily a relation between dancing and playing an instrument, since one can dance while singing without the need of an instrument.

Rabbi Moshe Feinstein, in his *Igrot Moshe*, also follows the opinion of the Rema. His reason is similar to the one we found in the Babylonian Talmud (*Beitzah* 30a) – as the custom of dancing on Shabbat and Holidays is well-established, "it is better for the people to do a transgression unintentionally than to do it knowingly".

On the other hand, Rabbi Ovadiah Yosef, an eminent Sephardic authority, forbids clapping hands and dancing on Shabbat and Holidays. In his opinion, all the Sephardim should follow this decree and act according to the decision of R. Joseph Karo, the author of the *Shulḥan Arukh*. The only holiday on which Rabbi Ovadiah Yosef allows dancing is *Simḥat Torah*.

The custom of dancing as an expression of joy on Shabbat and Holidays remains well-established. This becomes obvious when one visits the Western Wall in Jerusalem on any Friday night.

There is no particular position of the Conservative/Massorti Movement on this issue.

Rabbi Monique Susskind Goldberg
December 2005

FOR FURTHER READING

1. Allen, Wayne, *Perspectives on Jewish Law and Contemporary Issues*, Jerusalem, 2009, No. 28, pp. 142-152.

2. Feinstein, Moshe, *Responsa Igrot Moshe, Oraḥ Ḥayyim*, part 2, No. 100 [Hebrew].

3. Sperber, Daniel, *Sinai* 57 (5725), pp. 122-126 [Hebrew].

4. Yosef, Ovadiah, *Responsa Yeḥaveh Da'at*, vol. 2, No. 58 [Hebrew].

73. Is It Permissible to Use Public Transportation to Go to *Shul* on Shabbat?

QUESTION

Dear Rabbi,

I'm about a year away from starting college and I'm wondering about Jewish life there. The only *shul* within walking distance of the school I want to attend is Chabad-affiliated, which I don't think I would be entirely comfortable with. There is no Conservative *shul* close by. Although I am familiar with the debate over driving to *shul* on Shabbat, this is not actually an issue, since freshmen are not allowed to have cars on campus.

What I need to know is what is the *halakhah* regarding public transportation, if I were to take a bus to *shul* every Shabbat? I know it involves carrying money, but is that really so much worse than driving? Is there an alternative? Perhaps I should not consider this school, as there will be very few (if any) other *shomer Shabbat* Jews outside of the nearby Chabad? What are your thoughts?

ANSWER

Many modern halakhic authorities have dealt with the subject of using public transportation to go to synagogue on Shabbat (see Golinkin). A majority of them forbid it. Those who allow it add several conditions (see *Mishpetei Uzziel*):

1. The driver cannot be Jewish.

A Jewish driver would transgress Biblical and Rabbinic prohibitions:

a. When the motor of the bus is turned on, a spark is created, which is similar to kindling a fire. This is a Biblical prohibition (see Exodus 35:3 and *Mishnah Shabbat* 7:2).

b. The Rabbis have enacted several prohibitions [*shevut*] as a safeguard against the possibility of doing forbidden labor [*melakhah*] on Shabbat and Holidays (see for example *Beitzah* 36b; Maimonides, Laws of the Sabbath 23:4). Therefore they forbid using items or instruments on Shabbat and Holidays,

211

to avoid the possibility of being in a situation where the user needs to fix this instrument. Thus, it is a Rabbinic prohibition to drive a car (or a bus) on Shabbat to avoid a situation where the car breaks down and one would need to do some kind of repairs.

c. It is forbidden for a Jew to benefit from another Jew's transgression (see above, No. 67).

2. Most of the inhabitants of that city must be non-Jews.

A Jew is allowed to take advantage of an action prohibited on Shabbat performed by a non-Jew for himself or for other non-Jews, but not if this action is done for a Jew (see *ibid.* and *Orah Hayyim* 276:1-2). If most of the inhabitants of the city were Jewish, it would look as if the driver was driving the bus for them.

3. The vehicle must have regular stops. The reason is the same as the one above, that by making a special stop for a Jew, it is as if the driver is driving for him/her.

In some cases, for the sake of a *mitzvah*, *halakhah* permits a Jew to ask a non-Jew to do a Rabbinic prohibition in his stead (*Orah Hayyim* 586:21). For example, a Jew can ask a non-Jew to play an instrument on Shabbat (which is only a Rabbinic prohibition) for the *mitzvah* of honoring a bride and groom (*ibid.* 338:2). In our case, however, driving comprises not only Rabbinic prohibitions but also a Biblical prohibition (turning the motor on creates a spark). A Jew may not request a non-Jew to drive even if it is for the sake of the *mitzvah* of attending the Shabbat service in a synagogue.

4. You must be able to buy the ticket in advance.

Commercial transactions are forbidden on Shabbat (see *Beitzah* 37a and Rashi *ad loc., s.v. mishum mekah umimkar*). Therefore, money – which may not be used on Shabbat – is considered *muktzeh* [=set apart] and may not be carried (see Maimonides, Laws of the Sabbath 19:12; *Orah Hayyim* 303:22).

5. On Shabbat, it is forbidden to carry objects in the public domain (see *Oraḥ Ḥayyim* 301:7). For you to be able to carry the bus ticket, there should be an *eruv* around the city (to mark it as a private domain). Another option would be to carry the prepaid ticket attached to a piece of your clothing.

6. As it is forbidden to go more than 2,000 cubits (approximately one km.) outside the limits of your city on Shabbat (*Eruvin* 49b; Maimonides, *loc. cit.* 27:2), the bus should remain inside the limits of the city in which you live. This may be a problem if the synagogue you want to attend is in a city other than your college.

As you see, although it is technically possible to put all those conditions together, it is rather complicated and maybe you should think about other options:

a. Praying in a synagogue on Shabbat, although recommended (see Maimonides, Laws of Prayer and of the Priestly Blessing 8:1), is not mandatory. In order to keep Shabbat by not driving, you could pray by yourself at home, which can also be very beautiful and meaningful. Perhaps a few other Jewish students could be found as well, to pray together.

b. If you do want to be with a community for Shabbat prayers, you could pray on Shabbat and Holidays in the synagogue in which you do not feel so comfortable, and attend the Conservative *shul* on other occasions when it is permissible to drive or to take public transportation (weekday services, Purim, Ḥanukkah, weekday classes, etc.).

c. Finally, you could check whether there are other schools that offer the majors which you desire but also have more possibilities in terms of Jewish life and *shemirat Shabbat* [Sabbath observance].

Good luck in your studies.

Rabbi Monique Susskind Goldberg
January 2006

FOR FURTHER READING

1. Golinkin, David, "Riding to the Synagogue on Shabbat" in: *Responsa of the Va'ad Halakhah of the Rabbinical Assembly of Israel*, vol. 4 (5750-5752), pp. 16-32 [Hebrew with an English abstract; also available online at http://www.responsafortoday.com].

2. Uzziel, Ben-Zion Meir Ḥai, *Responsa Mishpetei Uzziel*, vol. 1, *Oraḥ Ḥayyim*, No. 9 [Hebrew].

3. For different reflections and reactions to the "Driving Teshuvah", see *Conservative Judaism* 56/3 (Spring 2004), pp. 21-50.

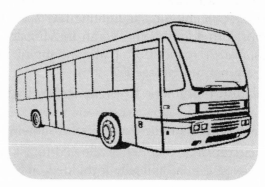

74. What Are the Conditions for Employing a *Shabbes Goy*?

QUESTION

Dear Rabbi,

How may a synagogue or an observant Jew employ a *Shabbes Goy*? It seems to me to be forbidden. Could you explain with citations in English?

ANSWER

In principle, you are right, it is a Rabbinic prohibition for a Jew to ask a non-Jew to do work on Shabbat in his stead (see *Shabbat* 150a; Maimonides, Laws of the Sabbath 6:1).

The reason given by Maimonides (*ibid.*) is that if a Jew has the work done by a non-Jew, he will take the laws of Shabbat lightly and will end up doing work himself.

There are two categories of labor forbidden on Shabbat: those that are a Torah prohibition, like lighting fire (see a list of the 39 types of labor forbidden by the Torah in *Mishnah Shabbat* 7:2; Maimonides, *ibid.* 7:1), and those that are Rabbinic prohibitions, like playing an instrument (see *ibid.* 23:4).

It is a Rabbinic prohibition to ask a non-Jew to do either kind of work.

There are exceptions to this rule in the following cases:

1. In some circumstances, a Jew is allowed to ask a non-Jew to do work, even if it is Biblically forbidden on Shabbat.

   a. For the sake of a sick person.

      For example, one can ask a non-Jew to light a fire for a sick Jew in cold weather (see *Oraḥ Ḥayyim* 328:17; *ibid.* 276:1). In very cold lands, one is even allowed to ask a non-Jew to light a fire on Shabbat for **any** Jew, because, "everyone can be considered sick when it is very cold" (*ibid.* 276:5).

   b. For relieving an animal from pain.

      For example, one may ask a non-Jew to milk the cows (see *ibid.* 305:20).

c. For the sake of saving Holy Scriptures.

One can ask a non-Jew to save sacred books from a fire on Shabbat (see *ibid.* 334:18).

2. Jewish Law permits a Jew to ask a non-Jew to do work that only falls under the category of Rabbinic prohibitions for the sake of doing a *mitzvah* [a commandment] (see *ibid.* 307:5).

For example, one can ask a non-Jew to play an instrument on Shabbat for the sake of rejoicing with the bride and groom (see *ibid.* 338:2).

Another example is related to the use of electricity. There is a discussion among the decisors as to whether using electricity on Shabbat is forbidden by the Torah (those who believe that using electricity is comparable to lighting a fire) or that it is only forbidden by Rabbinic decree (those who believe that electricity is not similar to lighting a fire).

Those who believe that the use of electricity is only a Rabbinic prohibition allow asking non-Jews to turn on lights, switch on heaters, and heat cooked food when it is for the sake of a *mitzvah*.

This applies to non-Jews working in the house or in the synagogue if the work they are asked to do is in the category of Rabbinic prohibitions, and if they do it for the sake of helping Jews observe *mitzvot* such as holding the Shabbat service, serving the Shabbat meal, etc.

I hope that I have managed to clarify this issue for you.

All the best,
Rabbi Monique Susskind Goldberg
May 2003

FOR FURTHER READING

Katz, Jacob, *The "Shabbes Goy": A Study in Halakhic Flexibility,* Philadelphia, 1989.

YOM KIPPUR

75. What Is the Origin of the *Viddui* in the Yom Kippur Service?

QUESTION

Dear Rabbi,

Could you please tell me when was the first time that the *Viddui* [Confession of Sins] was used in the Yom Kippur services? I believe that the first Yom Kippur was after Moses brought the second set of tablets down from the mountain. Is it possible that the *Viddui* was first used at that time or was it added later by the rabbis?

Thank you.

ANSWER

The earliest known formula of confession on Yom Kippur is that of the *Kohen Gadol* [the High Priest] in the Tabernacle. Regarding the confession in the Tabernacle, we read in Leviticus (16:21):

> And Aaron shall lay both his hands upon the head of the live goat, and confess over him all the iniquities of the Children of Israel, and all their transgressions, even all their sins...

The Bible does not specify the exact wording used by Aaron.

Regarding the High Priest's confession in the Temple service, the *Mishnah* is more precise:

> He came to his bullock.... And (the priest) pressed both his hands upon it and made confession. And thus he would say: "O Lord I have done wrong, I have transgressed, I have sinned before You, I and my house. Forgive the wrongdoings, the transgressions, the sins which I have committed and transgressed and sinned before You, I and my house, as it is written in the Torah of Moses Your servant: 'For on this day shall atonement be made for you'" (Leviticus 16:30). And they answered after him:

217

"Blessed be the Name of His glorious Kingdom for ever and ever" (*Mishnah Yoma* 3:8, 4:2 and 6:2).

In his book *The High Holy Days*, Rabbi Ḥayyim Kieval writes: "In the Second Commonwealth period, public confession of sins was an essential element in the liturgy of fast days" (p. 260). He gives Nehemia 9:2-3 as an example, but he adds that in the early synagogue there were no fixed words for *Viddui*. Even in the Yom Kippur service, each Jew confessed the specific sins he had committed during the past year. It is only in the first generation of *Amoraim* (ca. 225 CE) that we find specific formulas for *Viddui* (see *Yoma* 87b), and only in the late Amoraic and early Geonic period was the text expanded to what we know today.

Rabbi Monique Susskind Goldberg
October 2007

FOR FURTHER READING

1. Kieval, Ḥayyim Herman, *"Viddui* – The Confession of Sins" in: *The High Holy Days*, second revised and expanded edition, Jerusalem, 2004, pp. 257-263.

2. Marmorstein, Arthur, "The Confession of Sins for the Day of Atonement" in: Isidore Epstein *et al*, eds., *Essays in Honor of ... Dr. J. Hertz*, London, 1944, pp. 293-305.

SUKKOT

76. May One Eat in the *Sukkah* on *Shemini Atzeret/Simḥat Torah?*

QUESTION

Dear Rabbi,

What is the custom according to Conservative Judaism regarding eating in the *sukkah* on *Shemini Atzeret/Simḥat Torah* in the Diaspora? Is *kiddush* recited in the *sukkah* without the *berakhah leishev basukkah* [blessing for sitting in the *sukkah*] with the meal then eaten indoors, or are both *kiddush* and the meal taken in the *sukkah* without the *berakhah*? Alternatively, is the *sukkah* not used at all?

ANSWER

In ancient times, the beginning of the new month was set by witnesses who saw the new moon. Diaspora Jews did not always get the information on time and therefore were not sure on which day the festival should be celebrated. This is why, in the Diaspora, a second day was added to the festivals of Pesaḥ, Shavu'ot, Sukkot and Shemini Atzeret: *Yom Tov Sheni shel Galuyot* [the second day of the Diaspora]. These supplemental holidays are the second and eighth days of Pesaḥ, the second day of Shavu'ot, the second day of Sukkot and the second day of Shemini Atzeret, known in the Diaspora as Simḥat Torah.

Even though we now have a fixed calendar, Jews in the Diaspora still observe the ancestral custom of an extra holiday (see *Beitzah* 4b; Maimonides, Laws of Sanctification of the New Moon 5:5).

Shemini Atzeret is an independent holiday that follows the Sukkot holiday (Numbers 29:35 and elsewhere). Assuming there is a doubt about when Sukkot starts and when it ends, there is a possibility that Shemini Atzeret is actually the last day of Sukkot.

Therefore, it is not clear how to proceed regarding pronouncing the blessing on eating in the *sukkah* and saying *kiddush* for Shmini Atzeret. It would be contradictory to say the *kiddush* for

Shmini Atzeret yet bless the meal in the *sukkah* as though it were Sukkot.

Various customs have evolved that reflect a compromise to accommodate the fact that the eighth day might be Sukkot and is also Shmini Atzeret. Since a doubt remains that it may still be Sukkot, we eat in the *sukkah* without the corresponding blessing.

The most common practice is to say *kiddush* for Shemini Atzeret and have the meals in the *sukkah* both in the evening and in the morning, with the omission of the blessing on sitting in the *sukkah* (Maimonides, Laws of *Shofar, Sukkah* and *Lulav* 6:13; *Orah Hayyim* 668:1).

There are also other customs regarding having meals in the *sukkah* in the evening or in the daytime. All of them omit pronouncing the blessing *leishev basukkah* on Shemini Atzeret (see, for example, *Mahzor Vitri*, parag. 384). There is no particular Conservative custom.

On Simhat Torah in the Diaspora, it is certainly not necessary to eat in the *sukkah*; since it is already the 9th day since Sukkot began, there is no possibility that it is still Sukkot. Just as in Israel it is forbidden to eat in the *sukkah* on the eighth day because it would be an addition to the commandment to eat in the *sukkah* for seven days (see *Sukkah* 48a, and *Orah Hayyim*, 666:1), so in the Diaspora, where there is room for doubt regarding the eighth day, one can eat in the *sukkah*, but the ninth day would definitely be an addition.

Rabbi Diana Villa
October 2006

FOR FURTHER READING

1. *Entziklopedia Talmudit*, vol. 26, Jerusalem, 2004, *Yeshivat Sukkah*, column 39 [Hebrew].

2. Klein, Isaac, *A Guide to Jewish Religious Practice*, New York, 1992, p. 169.

3. "Leaving the *Sukkah* (without creating an uproar)", http:// www.ou.org/chagim/shmini-simchat/solong.htm

77. May One Put the *Skhakh* on Top of Stained or Painted Wooden Beams?

QUESTION

Dear Rabbi,

Is it acceptable to place the *skhakh* of a *sukkah* on top of wooden beams that are stained with wood stain or painted?

ANSWER

Like the *skhakh* itself, a beam supporting it must have three characteristics:

1. It must be grown from the earth (see *Orah Hayyim* 629:1);
2. It must be cut from its roots (*ibid.*);
3. It cannot be made from a material or from an object that receives impurity (see *ibid* 629:1, 7; and *Magen Avraham* subparag. 9).

If the beams were never used for another purpose, there is no problem supporting your *skhakh* on them. Painting them is not an issue.

Hag Sameah,

Rabbi Monique Susskind Goldberg
August 2007

PESAḤ

78. May One Drink White Wine at the *Seder* Table?

QUESTION

Dear Rabbi,

With Pesaḥ coming up, my question involves using white wine at the *Seder*.

I know that red wine is recommended. From what I can determine, there is a red wine/blood connection. Because of the blood that was put on the doorposts and the blood of the first plague, many authorities say that only red wine should be used at the *Seder*.

I also know that at various times in our history, white wine was used because of Blood Libel accusations. I assume that when white wine was used, the red wine/blood connection was ignored.

At my *Seder*, we use both red and white wines. To me, having a nice kosher wine is the important part, and the color really isn't important. Because of the strong connection in Christianity between wine and blood, I feel very uncomfortable making any connection between blood and red wine.

ANSWER

It is a *mitzvah* to try to obtain red wine for the *Seder* (see Jerusalem Talmud, *Pesaḥim*, 10:1, 37c and Babylonian Talmud, *Pesaḥim* 108b). If a person obtains white wine of a better quality, it may be used in lieu of red wine (see *Oraḥ Ḥayyim* 472:11).

R. Yitzḥak of Vienna offers various reasons for preferring red wine, among them: it reminds us of the blood of the Jewish children killed by Pharaoh and it reminds us of the Paschal sacrifice (see *Or Zaru'a*, part 2, *Hilkhot Pesaḥim*, parag. 256). However, wherever it is dangerous to drink red wine, for example, in times of blood libels, it is preferable to use white wine (see *Oraḥ Ḥayyim* 472, *Taz* subparag. 9 and *Mishnah Berurah* subparag. 38).

Red wine can also afford many teaching opportunities. The *Midrash* relates that when the Israelites crossed the Red Sea the angels started singing. God rebuked them saying: "My creatures are drowning in the sea and you are singing?!" We are reminded of the very important message that every human being's life is precious (see *Yalkut Shimoni, Ki Tavo* 1540 and parallel sources). A cup that is not full symbolizes that our happiness is not complete. Therefore, we remove or spill 16 drops of wine when we recite "Blood, fire and pillars of smoke", the Ten Plagues, and "*Detzakh Adash Be'aḥav*" (see Rema, *Oraḥ Ḥayyim* 473:7; Rabbi Menaḥem Mendl Kasher, *Haggadah Shleimah*, Jerusalem, 1967, pp. 126-127; Joshua Kulp and David Golinkin, *The Schechter Haggadah*, Jerusalem, 2009, pp. 47, 233). These drops would not be very noticeable with white wine.

In conclusion, red wine would be more traditional, though white wine of a higher quality can be used in lieu of red wine. Therefore, if drinking red wine at the *Seder* makes it difficult for you to concentrate on fulfilling this commandment, you can purchase an excellent Israeli white wine and thus be completely justified in your custom.

Happy Passover!

Rabbi Diana Villa

April 2008

FOR FURTHER READING

Hoffman, Lawrence and Arnow, David, *My People's Passover Haggadah*, Woodstock, Vermont, 2008, p. 58.

79. May One Eat Egg Matzah at the *Seder*?

QUESTION

Dear Rabbi,

I have a question about egg matzah. Do we still follow the *ḥumrah* [stringency] of not eating *matzah ashirah* [enriched matzah baked with fruit juice or eggs instead of water] on *Pesaḥ* because we are wary of the opinion in Jewish law which claims that fruit juices turn the flour into *ḥametz*, which cannot be eaten on Passover?

ANSWER

The *mitzvah* of eating matzah on the first night of *Pesaḥ* is not fulfilled with *matzah ashirah*, since we are told (Deuteronomy 16:3) to eat "unleavened bread, bread of distress" during Passover (see *Oraḥ Ḥayyim* 462:1).

Rabbi Joseph Karo allows eating *matzah ashirah* during *Pesaḥ* (see *ibid.*). However, the Rema (in his gloss on *Oraḥ Ḥayyim* 462:4), says that this is not the custom in Ashkenazic countries. The *Mishnah Berurah ad loc.* (subparagraph 15) explains that this prohibition of *matzah ashirah* throughout *Pesaḥ* is due to those decisors who hold that fruit juices ferment, and also because there might be some water mixed with the fruit juice, and that surely ferments.

So, if you follow the Ashkenazic *ḥumrah*, you may not eat *matzah ashirah*, yet Rabbi Joseph Karo and Sephardic decisors up to our day, like Rabbi Ovadiah Yosef, allow it (see *Yabi'a Omer*, part 1, *Oraḥ Ḥayyim*, No. 16).

It is interesting to note that the Rema allows *matzah ashirah* for old and sick people (*loc. cit.*), which means that he definitely does not consider it *ḥametz*.

Happy Passover!

Rabbi Diana Villa
April 2005

80. Why Do We Wash Our Hands and Then Eat *Karpas* During the *Seder*?

QUESTION

Dear Rabbi,

I am creating my own *Haggadah* and after doing some research. I came up with two questions on *Urehatz* and *Karpas* . I wanted to know if you would be able to answer them for me.

Urehatz:

I read in a commentary on the *Haggadah* that the ceremony of *Urehatz* [washing the hands before eating the *Karpas*] at the beginning of the *Seder* was instituted to teach the children about the laws of purification from *tum'ah* [impurity]. Why did the Rabbis feel the need to have the children become curious and ask questions at the *Seder* about this particular topic of impurity and not pick some other topic? What does that have to do with the *Seder*?

Karpas:

I read also that according to Rashi, there is a connection between the *Karpas* we use at the *Seder* and the striped coat Jacob gave to his son Joseph. How did the *Karpas* from the *Seder* go from a coat to a vegetable? When and why was this switch made?

ANSWER

Here are some answers to your *Seder* questions:

1. *Urehatz* and *Karpas*

It is true that at the *Seder* we do unusual things so that the children should stay awake and ask questions (see *Pesahim* 109a). However, that is **not** why we eat *Karpas* dipped in salt water at the *Seder*.

We do so because the *Seder* is modeled on the Greek *symposium* or banquet which always began with "appetizers", vegetables dipped in salt water or vinegar (see *Pesahim* 114a; *The Schechter Haggadah*, p. 183; Golinkin; Stein). According to *halakhah*, hands are always assumed to be impure unless they have been purified. When hands become damp, they can transmit impurity to the food. This is why one is required to wash the hands in order to purify them before dipping food in liquid (see *Oraḥ Ḥayyim* 158:4).

2. *Karpas* and Joseph's Coat

a. The word *Karpas* meaning a vegetable does not appear in the Bible. It appears in Talmudic sources, not in the context of Passover or the *Seder* night, but in the description of plants growing near water (see *Mishnah Shevi'it* 9:1; *Tosefta Kil'ayim* 1:1; *Sukkah* 39b).

The word *Karpas* comes from the Persian word *karafs* meaning "parsley", or from the Greek *karpos* "fruit of the soil".

The first time we see the word *Karpas* as representing one of the steps of the order of the *Seder* is in Rashi's time (11th century; see *Mahzor Vitry, Hilkhot Pesaḥ*, p. 281, parag. 65). But already in the time of the *Geonim* we find *Karpas* on a list of vegetables eaten at the beginning of the *Seder* (see *Seder Rav Amram Gaon*, ed. Goldschmidt, p. 112).

b. The word *Karpas* does appear in the Bible in the book of Esther (1:6) with the meaning of "fine silk" (see Ibn Ezra's commentary on this verse; see also Jastrow, who writes that this words comes from Sanskrit). The word *karpas* in the book of Esther is also explained by the Rabbis as an abbreviation of "pillows made of striped material" [*karim shel passim*] (see *Megillah* 12a).

Rashi in his commentary on Genesis makes the connection between Joseph's coat and the *Karpas* in Esther. He explains that Joseph's "striped coat" (*ketonet passim*) was made from fine silk like the *Karpas* described in the book of Esther (see Rashi on Genesis 37:3, *s.v. passim*).

We now see the connection between the word *Karpas* and Joseph's coat. Because of this coat showing their father's favoritism for Joseph, his brothers became jealous of him, sold him to Egypt and dipped the coat in blood so that Jacob would believe he was killed by an animal (Genesis 37:31-36). The

Talmud stresses the connection between this event and the fact that the Israelites went down to Egypt (see *Shabbat* 10b).

Once the connection between the word *Karpas* and Joseph's coat was made, it seems natural that some commentators of the *Haggadah* would add this explanation as to why we eat *Karpas* at the beginning of the *Seder*.

R. Manoaḥ of Narbonne made such a comment and explicitly pointed to the connection between the *Karpas* on the *Seder* plate and Joseph's striped garment:

> And we have the custom of *Karpas* as a reminder of the striped garment which Jacob our forefather made for Joseph, and which was the indirect cause for our fathers to go down into Egypt (*Sefer Hamenuḥah* on Maimonides, Laws of Leaven and Unleavened Bread 8:2, ed. Frankel, p. 343).

Although there are many more *midrashim* about the reason we eat *Karpas* at the beginning of the *Seder*, it seems very appropriate to begin the *Seder* with a reference to Joseph's coat dipped in blood, which was an indirect cause for the descent of the Israelites to Egypt.

Rabbi Monique Susskind Goldberg
March 2008

FOR FURTHER READING

1. Gevaryahu, Gilad J. and Wise, Michael L., "Why does the *Seder* begin with *Karpas*?", *Jewish Bible Quaterly* 27/2 (1999), pp. 104-111.

2. Golinkin, David, *Insight Israel: The View from Schechter*, second series, Jerusalem, 2006, p. 71.

3. Jastrow, Marcus, *A Dictionary of the Targumim, the Talmud Babli and Yerushalmi, and the Midrashic Literature*, Philadelphia, 1903, p. 673, *s.v. Karpas*.

4. Kulp, Joshua and Golinkin, David, *The Schechter Haggadah: Art, History and Commentary*, Jerusalem, 2009, p. 183.

5. Stein, Siegfried, *The Journal of Jewish Studies* 8 (1957), pp. 13-44.

6. See also http://www.balashon.com/2006/04/karpas.html

YOM HA'ATZMAUT

81. What Is the Attitude of the Conservative Movement to *Yom Ha'atzmaut*?

QUESTION

Dear Rabbi,

I am an emissary for the *Masorti* [Israeli Conservative Movement] in North America.

I was wondering if you can advise me about the Conservative Movement's position on *Yom Ha'atzmaut* [Israel Independence Day]. What I mean is: do we consider it a religious holiday? Where do we see God's presence in this holiday? Do we require the recitation of *Hallel* and a festive service on *Yom Ha'atzmaut*? I would appreciate it if you could direct me to the most relevant sources on this issue and to *responsa*, if any were written in the past.

ANSWER

The creation of the State of Israel was a turning point in our nation's history. After the *Shoah*, the Jewish people needed a homeland in which they could always find a safe haven, in which Jews from all over the world could come together, have political independence and sovereignty. The State could become a cultural and spiritual center as in ancient times.

There is a religious dimension to this historical event. The Jewish people prayed for 2,000 years for the return to this land in general and to Jerusalem in particular. Some examples in the Amidah prayer (which is recited three times a day) are:

> And to Jerusalem, Thy city, return in mercy, and dwell therein as Thou hast spoken... and speedily set up the throne of David.
> And let our eyes behold thy return in mercy to Zion.

This yearning is also expressed in the Passover *Seder*'s "Next year in Jerusalem". The Bible includes many verses, in particular in prophetic texts, in which these feelings and the centrality of

229

Jerusalem are expressed as well. See for example: "For out of Zion shall go forth the law and the word of the Lord from Jerusalem" (Isaiah 2:3 and Micah 4:2); "Your sons come from afar and your daughters are borne on the side" (prophecy on Jerusalem, Isaiah 60:4); "For Zion's sake I will not hold my peace, and for Jerusalem's sake I will not rest, until her triumph go forth as brightness, and her salvation as a torch that burns" (*ibid.* 62:1).

The creation of the State of Israel is, in the opinion of many, the fulfillment of a vision. The prayer for the well-being of the State of Israel calls it the "beginning of the blossoming of our redemption". Many people see it as a major miracle in our day.

Israel's Chief Rabbinate (Orthodox) established that on *Yom Ha'atzmaut* the *Hallel* should be recited (with or without the accompanying blessing) as on other holidays and a special *Haftarah* (reading from the Prophets) should be read. These special additions are included in Orthodox prayer books printed in Israel such as *Siddur Rinat Israel* and in some Orthodox prayer books printed abroad (Art Scroll, Chief Rabbi Sacks).

The *Kibbutz Hadati* (Modern Orthodox Kibbutz Movement) also introduced a special version of *Al Hanissim*. Neither the Chief Rabbinate nor the *Kibbutz Hadati* added a special Torah reading.

Conservative rabbis dealt in the 1960s with the need to celebrate Independence Day in our congregations, though they didn't decide on a definite pattern for the celebration (see Golinkin).

Sim Shalom, the Conservative prayer book, does not include a separate section for *Yom Ha'atzmaut*, but it indicates in the appropriate sections that *Al Hanissim* and Torah and *Haftarah* readings are to be included on this occasion.

In *Va'Ani Tefilati*, the Israeli Conservative prayer book, you will see relevant prayers and texts for study, based on a special booklet published by the *Masorti* Movement and the Israeli Rabbinical Assembly. It indicates that on Independence Day evening, after a festive service, *Hallel* is prayed, as well as other liturgical texts such as the *Sheheheyanu* blessing, the blowing of the *shofar*, and saying "Next year in rebuilt Jerusalem". In the morning, *Hallel* is said, and Torah and *Haftarah* portions are included. A festive meal is also recommended. A version of *Al Hanissim* for this holiday is included in the *Amidah* and Grace after meals as well.

I hope that you can plan a proper Independence Day service on the basis of these suggestions.

Ḥag Sameaḥ!

Rabbi Diana Villa

April 2004

FOR FURTHER READING

1. Ahrend, Aaron, *Israel's Independence Day: Studies*, Ramat Gan, 1998 [Hebrew].

2. Golinkin, David, ed., *Proceedings of the Committee on Jewish Law and Standards 1927-1970*, Jerusalem, 1997, pp. 476, 506, 513-514, 572, 585.

3. *Heichal Shlomo, Luaḥ Dinim Uminhagim Lishnat Tashsat*, Jerusalem, 2008, p. 75 [Hebrew].

4. *The Koren Sacks Siddur*, Jerusalem, 2009, pp. 910-922.

5. Rakover, Naḥum, *Hilkhot Yom Ha'atzmaut V'yom Yerushalayim*, second edition, Jerusalem, 1985 [Hebrew].

6. *Seder Tefillot Leyom Ha'atzmaut*, third edition, HaKibbutz Hadati, 1976 [Hebrew].

7. *Siddur Kol Ya'akov*, The Complete Artscroll Siddur, third edition, New York, 1995.

8. *Siddur Rinat Israel*, Ashkenaz, Jerusalem, 1983, pp. 437-443 [Hebrew].

9. *Siddur Sim Shalom*, a Prayerbook for Shabbat, Festivals and Weekdays, Jules Harlow, ed., New York, 1985, pp. 205-208.

10. *Siddur Sim Shalom for Weekdays*, New York, 2002, pp. 205-208.

11. *Siddur Va'ani Tefilati,* Simchah Roth, ed., Jerusalem, 1998, pp. 576-584 [Hebrew].

12. *Va'ani Tefillati: Siddur Yisraeli,* Tel Aviv, 2009, pp. 276-281 [Hebrew].

TISH'AH B'AV

82. How Should Mourning Be Observed During the Three Weeks Preceding the Ninth of Av?

QUESTION

Dear Rabbi,

Please clarify the parameters of mourning observance during the three weeks preceding *Tish'ah B'Av* with regard to the following points:

1. Is recorded music allowed or is it considered the same as live music?

2. Are regularly scheduled ballet lessons for children allowed? What about for adults?

3. Is swimming prohibited only beginning on *Rosh Ḥodesh Av* or during the entire three weeks or is it permissible? What about kids' swimming lessons?

ANSWER

The three weeks you allude to are the weeks between the fast of the Seventeenth of Tammuz, which marks the day when the walls of the city of Jerusalem were breached, and the Ninth of Av, when the Temple was destroyed both by the Babylonians in 586 BCE and by the Romans in 70 CE. As a result, mourning customs are observed during this period to mark the Temple's destruction.

According to the Talmud, the mourning customs apply only to the week of *Tish'ah B'av* itself (*Ta'anit* 29b). The Talmud forbids getting haircuts and washing clothes during that week, but it forbids eating meat and drinking wine only on the eve of *Tish'ah B'av* itself. The *Shulḥan Arukh* adds the prohibition of wearing new clothes and bathing and extends the prohibition to consuming meat and drinking wine to the whole week (*Oraḥ Ḥayyim* 551:3, 9, 16).

Some decisors rule that the following mourning customs apply during the nine days beginning on the first of *Av*: not

233

getting married (*ibid.*, parag. 2), not eating meat or drinking wine (*ibid.*, parag. 9), not washing clothes nor wearing new clothes (the Rema, *ibid.*, parags. 3 and 6), and not bathing (*ibid.*, parag. 16).

Ashkenazic Jews extended the following mourning customs to the three weeks beginning on the Seventeenth of Tammuz: not getting married (the Rema, *ibid.*, parag. 2), not getting haircuts and not wearing new clothes (see the 19th century code, *Ḥayyei Adam*, 133:8). Sephardic Jews are warned not to eat new fruit or wear new clothes during the Three Weeks as well (see *Oraḥ Ḥayyim* 551:17).

One should refrain from live music during the Three Weeks. Some rule that singing without music is allowed (see *Responsa Igrot Moshe, Yoreh De'ah* 2:137; *Yeḥaveh Da'at* 6:34). Some do not allow singing altogether (see *Responsa Tzitz Eliezer* 15:33), while other authorities take a lenient position and allow listening to recorded music during these days (see Melamed). The reason for this is apparently that listening to recorded music is so commonplace today, that it is not considered particularly joyful or celebratory.

Sephardic Jews allow even live music for circumcision and *Bar Mitzvah* parties, as well as at weddings that take place up to *Rosh Ḥodesh Av* (see *Yeḥaveh Da'at, loc. cit.*).

As far as ballet and swimming lessons, stopping for three weeks would potentially be detrimental to the children's practice. Since classes are ongoing, serve an educational purpose, and are not merely for pleasure, they should be allowed except on *Tish'ah B'Av* itself (see *Responsa Rav Pe'alim*, part 4, *Oraḥ Ḥayyim*, No. 29).

Rabbi Diana Villa
August 2006

FOR FURTHER READING

1. Gartner, Ya'akov, *Gilgulei Minhag B'olam Hahalakhah*, Jerusalem, 5755, Chapters 1-2 [Hebrew].

2. Melamed, Eliezer, "Customs of the Three Weeks", http://www.yeshiva.org.il/midrash/shiur.asp?id=7966

THEOLOGY AND IDEOLOGY

83. Are Messianic Jews Considered Jewish?

QUESTION

Dear Rabbi,

Who are Messianic Jews? Are they really Jewish?

ANSWER

The people who call themselves Messianic Jews keep Jewish Laws (e.g., Shabbat and Holidays), but believe that Jesus is God and that he is the Messiah who already came and must return. There are both Jews and non-Jews in these groups.

The Jews who believe in Jesus have separated themselves from the Jewish people and are considered apostates. Judaism believes that a human being cannot be God, that there is *one* God and not three, and that the Messiah has not yet come.

Rabbi Monique Susskind Goldberg
August 2005

FOR FURTHER READING

1. Cohen Sherbok, Dan, *Messianic Judaism*, U.K., 2000.

2. "Messianic Judaism"
    http://en.wikipedia.org/wiki/Messianic_Judaism

84. May I Keep a Buddha Statuette in my Home?

QUESTION

Dear Rabbi,

Quite a number of years ago, when vacationing in Thailand, I bought a beautifully gilded statuette of the Buddha. I appreciated it as an artefact, for its aesthetic value. Over the years, I have defended my decision to keep it in my house, as an artefact, but I am growing more and more uncomfortable with it. On the one hand (as a cultural anthropologist), I do not want to close myself off to the artistic expressions of other cultures. On the other hand, I am aware of the fact that strictly speaking, it is an idol. What do you think? Can I keep it in my home?

ANSWER

According to *halakhah,* if an object is made in order to worship it, it is forbidden and must be destroyed (see *Avodah Zarah* 41a; *Yoreh De'ah* 141:1 and 146:14).

But if that object was made from the start with the unique intention of being a piece of art, there is no problem for you to keep it in your house (*Yoreh De'ah, ibid.*).

Buddha is not considered as a deity, he is venerated but not worshipped. The statuette is supposed to remind the faithful of his teachings so that they can live a better life. If that is so, there should be no problem keeping it in your home as a work of art.

Sincerely,

Rabbi Diana Villa
April 2005

85. May One Delete the Name of God From a Computer?

QUESTION

Dear Rabbi,

I am interested in responsa regarding deleting the name of God when writing on a computer.

ANSWER

According to *halakhah*, it is forbidden to erase the name of God. The rabbis derive this prohibition from Deuteronomy 12:2-4:

> You shall utterly destroy all the places in which the nations whom you are to dispossess serve their gods... and you shall overthrow their altars, and break their pillars... and destroy their name out of that place. You shall not do so to the Lord, your God.

In *Sifrei Deuteronomy* 61 (Finkelstein edition, p. 127) they learn that the words "You shall not do so to the Lord your God" mean not erasing His name.

In order to understand when one may be guilty of erasing God's name, we must first analyze what is defined halakhically as writing. Jewish law does not allow erasing that which it considers writing.

Writing appears in two different contexts in Jewish law – in the laws of Shabbat and in the laws of *gittin* [divorce writs].

In both contexts, writing is defined as something written with a durable material such as ink, that lasts over time (Maimonides, Laws of the Sabbath 11:15 and Laws of Divorce 4:1).

Letters on a computer screen are only magnetic signs that by electronic means become letters and words on the screen. These letters are not permanent. They only remain on the screen as long as the computer is on, and electricity makes it work, and even then they are actually being turned on and off every few seconds. The letters also disappear if we scroll down the screen and when we disconnect the computer.

This should be enough for us to prove that erasing any word on the computer screen, including God's name, would not be considered erasing according to Jewish law.

Furthermore, the person who is writing on the computer does not intend for the letters to stay on the screen permanently. Therefore, there is no sanctification of words when writing on a computer (see *Responsa Maharit*, vol. 2, *Oraḥ Ḥayyim*, No. 3, who explains that only writing which is valid for writing a divorce writ is sanctified and therefore cannot be erased).

The Talmud, *Megillah* 32a teaches: "Rav Matna said: The *luḥot* and the podium do not have any sanctity". According to Maimonides (Laws of *Tefillin, Mezuzah* and the Scroll of the Law 10:4), the *luḥot* are chalkboards, used to teach children. Rabbi Isaac Elḥanan Spektor (*Responsa Ein Yitzḥak*, part 1, *Oraḥ Ḥayyim*, No. 5) proves from this that if there is no intent for the writing to be permanent, it lacks sanctity.

Some authorities are stricter (see the *Responsa of Tashbetz*, part 1, No. 2). The Bar Ilan Responsa project, for example, prints ידוד instead of the Tetragrammaton in Biblical verses, ostensibly so that no one will have qualms about deleting or even exiting from a text which includes God's name.

In our opinion it is not necessary to be strict regarding erasing words on the computer screen, including the name of God.

Sincerely,

Rabbi Diana Villa
March 2003

86. Is a Snowman an Idol?

QUESTION

Dear Rabbis,

Is there a problem of idolatry when constructing a snowman? Please provide sources so I can explain to my kids what we are doing.

ANSWER

No, there is no idolatry problem when constructing a snowman.

According to *halakhah*, it is only forbidden to build a statue if it is made in order to worship it (see *Avodah Zarah* 41a; *Yoreh De'ah* 141:1).

Have fun with your kids!

Rabbi Monique Susskind Goldberg
December 2008

87. Is It Permissible to Bow to a Photograph?

QUESTION

Dear Rabbi,

My family currently lives in Japan. My son attends a martial arts program here as he had for some years in the United States. At the start and close of the class it is customary for participants to bow to each other, as is the common custom in this country. We have never had any problem with this.

However, at the start and close of the class, participants not only bow to each other but also bow in respect toward a photograph on a wall of the founder of that martial art. They are sitting on their knees on a canvas or straw mat when they do this.

My son said that he could not do that without consulting our proper religious authorities. He was told that it was disrespectful to stand out when everyone shows respect to the founder of the school and that he could not train there if that were the case. So, he is not training there for now. This has been a big blow.

We do not feel that there is *avodah zarah* [idolatry] intention in this, but we want to know what the *halakhah* requires in this situation. Is bowing toward a photograph really a problem or is it nothing to be concerned about? We feel: "better safe than sorry".

What does *Hashem* [God] expect of us in this situation – could you please advise us? This is a very important issue to us.

Thanks in advance.

ANSWER

Bowing to a person is not forbidden. According to *Sanhedrin* 61b:

> *'Thou shalt not bow down thyself to them'*[to an idol] (Exodus 20:5) – thou mayest not bow down to them, but thou mayest bow down to a human being like thyself.

The Talmud then explains that it is only forbidden to bow to a person if he considers himself a god (such as Haman), as idolatry may be involved.

Rabbi Joseph Karo rules in *Yoreh De'ah* 242:16 that one may bow to one's teacher as a form of respect.

Many people have pictures of rabbis on the walls. According to Rabbi Karo (*ibid.* 141:7), there is no problem having a picture portraying somebody's face on the wall. It follows that if one can bow to a person out of respect, and his picture is allowed on the wall, bowing to his picture is allowed as well.

Your son's class is not bowing to the photograph as a form of worship, but rather in respect to the founder of that martial art. Therefore, this ritual should not be a problem and your son should be able to return to his training.

Sincerely,

Rabbi Diana Villa
February 2006

FOR FURTHER READING

Yosef, Ovadiah, *Responsa Yeḥaveh Da'at*, vol. 3, No. 63 [Hebrew].

WOMEN

88. May Women Wear *Tefillin*?

QUESTION

Dear Rabbi,

Is it halakhically permissible for women to wear *tefillin*? If so, why? If not, why not? I am writing a paper on women and *tefillin*.

ANSWER

Women are exempt from performing positive time-bound commandments (commandments that must be done at a specific time) (see *Mishnah Kiddushin* 1:7; *Kiddushin* 29a).[10]

The commandment of wearing *tefillin* is considered a positive time-bound commandment because one does not wear tefillin on Shabbat and holidays or at night (*Eruvin* 96a). In consequence, women are exempted from this obligation (see *Mishnah Berakhot* 3:3; *Berakhot* 20b; *Kiddushin* 34a; Maimonides, Laws of *Tefillin*, *Mezuzah* and the Scroll of the Law 4:13; *Oraḥ Ḥayyim* 38:3).

However, according to *halakhah*, a woman is not forbidden to perform positive time-bound commandments, and she may take them upon herself (see *Eruvin* 96a-b; Maimonides, Laws of *Tzitzit* 3:9; the Rema in *Oraḥ Ḥayyim* 17:2 and 589:6).

Therefore, a woman is halakhically permitted to wear *tefillin* (see *Mekhilta deRabbi Yishma'el*, *Masekhta dePasḥa*, Horowitz edition, p. 68; *Eruvin* 96a, where it is related that Michal, King Saul's daughter, wore *tefillin* and the Sages did not protest).[11]

The medieval authorities [*Rishonim*] are divided on the question whether a woman who performs a positive time-bound commandment is allowed to say the blessing accompanying it.

Rashi, Maimonides and R. Joseph Karo think that a woman who performs a commandment she is not obliged to perform,

---

10 R. David Abudraham (Spain, ca. 1340) suggested that this is because the Sages felt that their responsibilities within the home often precluded their ability to perform that class of *mitzvot* in a timely fashion.

11 See Golinkin, pp. 25-27, for a discussion of the different version found in the Palestinian Talmud.

should not say a blessing over it (see Maimonides, *ibid.*; *Oraḥ Ḥayyim* 589:6).

But many *Rishonim* such as Rabbeinu Tam, Rabbeinu Zeraḥyah Halevi Gerondi, the Rashba and others (see Golinkin, pp. 31 ff. for additional names), believe that women are allowed to say the blessing accompanying positive time-bound commandments. Rabbeinu Tam and Rashba explicitly mention the example of Michal Bat Shaul (see Rabbeinu Tam in *Tosafot Rosh Hashana* 33a, *s.v. ha*; *Responsa Rashba*, part 1, No. 123 and the Rema in *Oraḥ Ḥayyim, ibid*).

We do find some decisors who forbid women to wear *tefillin*. Yet it seems that all the opposition has its source in one sentence attributed to the Maharam of Rothenburg (d. 1293), where he says that women should not wear *tefillin* "because they do not know how to keep themselves clean"[12] (cited in *Sefer Hatashbetz*, parag. 270 and in *Orḥot Ḥayyim*, Laws of Tefillin, parag. 3, fol. 7b). The Rema codified this opinion in *Oraḥ Ḥayyim* 38:3,[13] and this was accepted by later authorities such as R. Abraham Gombiner in *Magen Avraham* (*ibid.*, subparag. 3) and R. Israel Meir HaKohen in *Mishnah Berurah* (*ibid.*, subparag. 13).

However, this opinion contradicts the Talmud and the *Rishonim* as we saw above, and there is no reason to accept an opinion stating that women are not able to keep their bodies clean. Even the *Magen Avraham*, who accepts the Maharam's opinion, adds that "if women were obliged to wear *tefillin* they would keep their bodies clean". In other words, there is no difference between men and women in this matter.

We can thus conclude that according to the Talmud and almost all the *Rishonim*, women are allowed to wear *tefillin*, and

---

12 Another version reads "pure" instead of "clean", but this would contradict the Talmudic passage "words of Torah are not susceptible to impurity". Cf. below, No. 89.

13 The Rema here contradicts his own statement in *Oraḥ Ḥayyim* 17:2 and 589:6 where, as we have seen above, he allows women to recite the blessings on positive time-bound commandments.

according to many, they are also allowed to say the blessings upon putting on the *tefillin*.

Rabbi Monique Susskind Goldberg
January, 2006

FOR FURTHER READING

Golinkin, David, "Women and *Tefillin*", in *The Status of Women in Jewish Law: Responsa*, Jerusalem, 2001, pp. 23-45 [Hebrew with an English abstract]. For an English translation of this *responsum*, see *Conservative Judaism* 50/1 (Fall 1997), pp. 3-18.

89. Is It Forbidden for Menstruating Women to Wear *Tefillin*?

QUESTION

Dear Rabbi,

I have read that one should refrain from wrapping *tefillin* if "you are suffering from an 'involuntary bodily secretion' (solids, liquids, or gaseous)". Does this mean that women should refrain from wrapping *tefillin* while menstruating?

ANSWER

Halakhah does not provide a direct answer to your question since most women did not wear *tefillin* in the past, but we can deduce the answer from the law concerning a menstruating woman and a *Sefer Torah*.

A menstruating woman is included in the list of people who are impure and therefore are forbidden to enter the Temple (Leviticus 15:19; cf. below, No. 92).

However, it is clearly stated in the Talmud, that an impure person can read or learn Torah because "words of Torah are not susceptible to impurity" (*Berakhot* 22a).

Maimonides, following this statement, rules that an "impure" person like a menstruating woman can touch a Torah scroll, because a Torah does not receive impurity (Laws of *Tefillin Mezuzah* and the Scroll of the Law 10:8). In that same law, Maimonides distinguishes between "impurity" and uncleanness. There is no problem for a ritually impure person to touch a Torah scroll if his/her hands are clean (*ibid.*).

The *Shulḥan Arukh* concurs (*Yoreh De'ah* 282:9). Menstruation is not uncleanness. The woman is impure but clean.

In conclusion, a woman can continue to put on *tefillin* or to read from the Torah even during menstruation.

Rabbi Monique Susskind Goldberg
March 2006

FOR FURTHER READING

1. See above, No. 88.

2. Villa, Diana and Susskind Goldberg, Monique, "The Distancing of Menstruants From the Synagogue and Sacred Rites", *To Learn and To Teach*, No. 5, Jerusalem, 2007.

90. May Women Read Torah and *Haftarah*?

QUESTION

Dear Rabbi,

Shalom. I have a question and I understand that it might be difficult for you to address it because of some very profound differences in the orientation of the Orthodox position and the Conservative position. However, I do need guidance on this question.

I attend a Conservative synagogue. My Rabbi of forty years has retired with his wife to live in Jerusalem. This is a blessing for them, but less so for me. This is because the Rabbi – on almost all questions – leaned towards the Orthodox position. For example, at a *Bat Mitzvah* ceremony, girls read *Haftarah*, but could not say the preliminary and concluding blessings; neither were they permitted to read Torah. Now we have a new Rabbi and the winds of change are blowing. The new Rabbi will not permit the reading of Torah, but women will be allowed to say the blessings that precede and follow the *Haftarah*.

As a Jew who is becoming more observant, I need to know what I can and cannot accept. Some say that reading the *Haftarah* does not carry the same halakhic implication as does reading a Torah portion. Others say that women reading *Haftarah* is acceptable, but only as long as they do not recite the blessings preceding and following the *Haftarah*.

The halakhic decision of what women may do in this regard may be clear-cut, but what is not clear-cut are my personal issues. This is my parents' *shul*. My father, may he rest in peace, is remembered by many of the older congregants and this is the *shul* that I went to with him. This is also my mother's synagogue. I would hate to leave. But we all have our lines that we draw. Certainly I could not attend services where girls and women read Torah in mixed assembly with men. However, this issue of the *Haftarah* blessings is not as clear-cut. Or is it?

What can you offer in the way of advice? Thank you.

ANSWER

I can understand that you are in a difficult situation and that you will have to make some choices in order to feel comfortable in the synagogue you attend. The information I can give you is only about the halakhic question of Torah (or *Haftarah*) reading by women. Only you can decide how you will feel about this information.

Firstly, it must be stressed that there is no difference between the reading and the blessings. In the time of the *Tannaim* (ca. 70-200 CE), whoever went up to the Torah read his portion, the first reader said the opening blessing and the last reader said the closing blessing after he finished his reading (see *Mishnah Megillah* 4:1). In Talmudic times, it was accepted that every person who read Torah would say a blessing before and after the reading (see *Megillah* 21b). Only in the Middle Ages, when most of the people who went up to the Torah could not read the verses from the parchment with the appropriate cantillation, did a new custom emerge: one person who was an expert in Torah reading (the *ba'al keriah*) would read the entire portion, and this is the common Ashkenazic custom until today (at Sephardic synagogues, many people still read their own *aliyot*). The one who is offered an *aliyah* to the Torah says the blessings before and after the reading of his portion, and when he can, he reads in a low voice together with the reader. From these facts we learn that there is no halakhic difference between the one who recites the blessings and the one who reads the Torah. Whoever is permitted by *halakhah* to read from the Torah is also permitted to recite the blessing or vice versa.

The second important thing to take into account is that the obligation of reading the Torah is not an obligation for each individual. The obligation falls on the community, which is obliged to make the Torah heard in public (see Maimonides, Laws of Prayer and of the Priestly Blessing 12:1). The commandment is that the Torah should be read. This is why, according to many authorities, it really does not matter who reads and it may even be a minor (see, for example, the Meiri,

Beit Habehirah to *Megillah* 24a, ed. Hershler, Jerusalem, 1962, p. 79).

We read in the Talmud: "Everyone goes up to read among the seven, even a woman, even a minor" (*Megillah* 23a). This *baraita* fits in with what we said above; the obligation of reading the Torah is not an individual obligation, it is the community's obligation. This is why it does not matter who goes up to read. It is only later that the Sages added a sentence to the *baraita* "that a woman should not read from the Torah because of *kevod tzibbur*" [the honor of the congregation] (*ibid.*). In other words, it was a "disgrace and an embarrassment" to the congregation if women read from the Torah, because this would shame the men since people would say that the men do not know how to read (see Tosefta *Megillah* 3:11-12, Lieberman edition, p. 356; *Responsa Tzitz Eliezer*, part 20, No. 36). But today, men and women receive equal educational opportunities, and the original reason for not allowing women to read from the Torah no longer exists.

Thus, halakhically, women are permitted to read from the Torah and/or to have *aliyot*. As we have seen, this includes the blessings.

If women are permitted to read the Torah with the blessings, it is evident that they are also permitted to read the *Haftarah* with the blessings, because most authorities rule that even a minor can read the *Haftarah* with the blessings (*Megillah* 24a; *Orah Hayyim* 284:4). According to Rabbi Ovadiah Yosef, the obligation for reading the *Haftarah* is not on the same level as the obligation for reading the Torah. The Torah reading is a Biblical commandment (see Maimonides, *ibid.* 12:1), but the reading of the *Haftarah* is, according to Rabbi Ovadiah Yosef, only "honor we give to the prophets" (*Yehaveh Da'at*, part 1, No. 85).

In conclusion, women are permitted by *halakhah* to be called to the Torah and to say the blessings before and after the reading, and they are also allowed to read the *Haftarah* and to say the blessings accompanying it.

I know that this answer does not solve your problem, because you feel more comfortable praying in a more Orthodox environment, and your feelings should be respected. But it is also legitimate, halakhically speaking, for your new Rabbi to let girls and women say the blessings with the *Haftarah*, and I suppose that, in time, your congregation will eventually evolve into a more egalitarian community and call women to the Torah.

Now the choice is yours. Either you will feel more at ease with your new Rabbi's approach, knowing that it is permissible for women to go up to the Torah and read the *Haftarah* with the blessings, or you will decide that it is preferable for you to look for another place to pray, where the customs with which you are familiar are adhered to.

I hope I was able to help you in this difficult decision.

Rabbi Monique Susskind Goldberg

FOR FURTHER READING

1. Golinkin, David, "*Aliyot* for Women" in: *The Status of Women in Jewish Law: Responsa*, Jerusalem, 2001, pp. 83-108 [Hebrew with an English abstract].

2. Susskind Goldberg, Monique, and Villa, Diana "*Aliyot* for Women", *To Learn and To Teach*, No. 2, Jerusalem, 2004.

91. May Women Wear a *Tallit Katan*?

QUESTION

Dear Rabbi,

Is it halakhicaly permissible for women to wear a *tallit katan* [small *tallit* with *tzitzit* worn under the clothing] ? If so, why? If not, why not?

ANSWER

The Torah explicitly commands that *tzitzit* be attached to four-cornered garments (see Numbers 15:38-39). The function of the fringes is to remind the wearer of the *mitzvot* (*ibid.*). This *mitzvah* was codified in Maimonides, Laws of *Tzitzit* and in *Oraḥ Ḥayyim*, paragraphs 8-24.

However, the *mitzvah* of wearing *tzitzit* is not an obligation in the full sense of the word. The law is that when a person wears a garment with four corners, this garment requires *tzitzit* on each of those corners (see Maimonides, Laws of *Tzitzit* 3:1; *Oraḥ Ḥayyim* 9:1). Nevertheless, it is not an obligation to wear such a four-cornered garment.

Originally, the *tzitzit* were put on everyday men's cloaks, which were like big shawls with four corners (resembling the *abayah* of the Beduin). When those cloaks went out of fashion and men no longer wore four-cornered garments, the use of shawls with *tzitzit* became restricted to prayer time and became "prayer shawls" or *tallitot*.

The custom of wearing a small four-cornered garment under the outer clothing then arose, in order to fulfill the commandment of *tzitzit* and to be reminded of the *mitzvot* all day long (see *Oraḥ Ḥayyim* 24:1). This is the *tallit katan* (see *ibid.* 8:3 and above, No. 35).

As *tzitzit* are worn only in day time, wearing *tzitzit* is considered a positive time-bound commandment and, in consequence, women are not obligated to do it. However, as in the case of other positive time-bound commandments, women are permitted to wear *tzitzit* (see Maimonides, *ibid.* 3:9; *Orah Hayyim* 17:2).

According to Maimonides, if women wear *tzitzit*, they should do so without saying a blessing (Maimonides, *ibid.*); however, the Rema holds that women may recite the blessings on positive time-bound commandments (*Orah Hayyim, ibid.* in the Rema). In this regard, the Rema rules like Rabbeinu Tam in the *Tosafot* (*Rosh Hashanah* 33a, *s.v. ha*) and the Rosh (*Kiddushin*, chap. 1, parag. 49).

But the Rema adds in the same paragraph, following the *Maharil* and the *Agur*, that a woman should not wear *tzitzit* since it appears like boastfulness, since even men are not required to wear *tzitzit* unless they are wearing a four-cornered garment. However, this is a late opinion which is contradicted by the Talmud (*Menahot* 43a) and the *Rishonim*.

In conclusion, there is no impediment for a woman to wear a *tallit* or a *tallit katan*. However, the choice to wear a *tallit katan* should not be for the sake of showing off or as feminist demonstration, but out of a sincere desire to perform this very important *mitzvah*.

Rabbi Monique Susskind Goldberg
July 2004

FOR FURTHER READING

1. Cayam, Aviva, in: Micah Halpern and Shana Safrai, eds. *Jewish Legal Writings by Women*, Jerusalem, 1998, pp. 119-142.

2. *Encyclopaedia Judaica*, second edition, Jerusalem, 2007, vol. 19, "*Tallit*", p. 406.

3. Feinstein, Moshe, *Igrot Moshe, Orah Hayyim*, part 4, No, 49 [Hebrew].

92. Why Do Some Men Refuse to Shake Women's Hands?

QUESTION

Dear Rabbi,

I recently attended a business meeting where a Jewish man was participating. When it came time for introductions, he would not shake the hand of women participants. I vaguely recall there being a religious reason for this, but cannot remember what it is. Can you help?

ANSWER

Many Orthodox men avoid physical contact with women in order to avoid any possible transgression. They are called *shomrei negiah*, i.e., those who guard against touching [women].

This prohibition of physical contact between the sexes has its origin in two different sets of laws:

1. Jewish Law forbids sexual relations between close family members (see Leviticus 18:6 and ff., 20:17 and ff.; *Even Ha'ezer* parag. 15) and between a man and a married woman (*ibid.* 17:1). These forbidden relations are called *issurei arayot*.

In order to avoid any risk of sexual relations with a person from these categories, *halakhah* forbids close physical contact [*keiruv basar*] with them (see Maimonides, Laws of Forbidden Sexual Relations 21:1; *Even Ha'ezer* 20:1 and 21:7).[14]

2. The second set of laws concern menstruating women. A woman is considered impure during the period around her menstruation; she is a *niddah*. Jewish Law forbids sexual intercourse with such a woman (see Leviticus 18:19; *Yoreh De'ah* 183:1 and the Rema there).

In order to avoid any possibility of sexual intercourse between husband and wife during the period when the woman is *niddah*, the authorities have established a list of *harhakot* or

---

14 This rule does not apply to a father and his daughter and a mother and her son who are allowed close physical contact, e.g., handshaking, hugging, etc. (see Maimonides *ibid.* 21:7).

restrictions to create a distance between them during that time period. They prohibit any physical contact between husband and wife; the husband cannot even touch his wife with his little finger (see Maimonides, *ibid.* 11:18-19; *Yoreh De'ah* 195).

People observing the laws of *negiah*, wanting to avoid any possible transgressions in the area of forbidden sexual relations, take on themselves the stringency of both sets of laws. Here is how Rabbi Moshe Feinstein, an ultra-Orthodox decisor, explains the reason for forbidding handshakes between men and women:

> To offer one's hand to a woman in the manner of those greeting others upon meeting – it is obvious that it is prohibited even for an unmarried woman since they are *niddah*, and how much the more so it is prohibited for a married woman (*Igrot Moshe, Orah Hayyim*, part 1, No. 113).

R. Moshe Feinstein's argument seems to be that it is forbidden for a man to shake a woman's hand because she is either married and part of the *issurei arayot*, or if she is not married, she is *niddah* (impure because of her menstruation).[15]

However these stringencies have no real basis in *halakhah*:

a. On the issue of the prohibition of touching close family members or married women, both Maimonides and the *Shulḥan Arukh* describe the way the touching occurs: *Derekh Ta'ava* "in a lustful manner"; *Neheneh bekeiruv bassar* "enjoying close physical contact" (see Maimonides, *ibid.* 21:1; *Even Ha'ezer* 20:1). They do not speak of mere touching but of touching with a sexual connotation. A handshake is certainly not what they had in mind.

b. On the issue of a *niddah*, we do not find in the main halakhic sources – *Mishnah*, Talmud, Maimonides or *Shulḥan Arukh* – a prohibition for a man to touch a woman during her menstruation outside of the context of sexual relations. The laws of distancing from such a woman are limited to her husband

---

15 As a non-married woman did not go to the ritual bath, she did not purify herself from her preceding menstruation.

with the clear goal of preventing sexual relations between a husband and wife.

However, we do find the custom of avoiding any contact with women during their menstruation principally in the eleventh and twelfth centuries among the *Hassidei Ashkenaz* and mystical circles. Being in any contact with a woman when she is *niddah* was considered dangerous. Those groups were probably influenced by the *Baraita D'Masekhet Niddah*, written by a sectarian group in Israel in the sixth or seventh century. According to this *Baraita*, it is dangerous for anyone to have any physical contact with a *niddah*, including eating the food she prepares (see *To Learn and To Teach*, No. 5, pp. 18-19). None of this appears in the authoritative sources of *halakhah*.

We therefore see that the *shomrei negiah* are taking upon themselves stringencies that are not required by Jewish Law.

This explains the fact that there are different opinions among halakhic authorities on the question whether one can return a handshake from the opposite sex in public events or business situations. Rabbi Feinstein himself, in another *responsum*, shows some sympathy for those people that do shake hands. He writes:

> Concerning that which you saw people being lenient even those who are *yir'ei shamayim* [Godfearing] – to offer their hand to a woman when she stuck her hand out. Perhaps they reasoned that this is not *derekh ḥibah* [affection] and *ta'avah* [lust] – but this is difficult to rely on (see *Igrot Moshe, Even Ha'ezer*, part 1, No. 56).

Rabbi Feinstein acknowledges that there are circumstances where the issue of *negiah* [touching] is not so problematic, such as in situations where there is clearly no sexual lust involved. He is also aware that there are observant men who do shake hands with women in situations where there is no sexual connotation to this act. Although Rabbi Feinstein does not accept this, he thinks that one should not judge such people (see *ibid.* and also part 4, No. 32, parag. 9).

Some Orthodox authorities find room for leniency for the sake of not embarrassing the woman who extends her hand (see for instance the opinion of Rabbi Yehudah Henkin).

I hope I have helped you to understand the behavior of the person at your meeting.

Rabbi Monique Susskind Goldberg

FOR FURTHER READING

1. Epstein, Louis, *Sex Laws and Customs in Judaism*, New York, 1948, pp. 110-112.

2. Feinstein, Moshe, *Igrot Moshe, Even Ha'ezer*, part 1, No. 56, last paragraph; *ibid.*, part 2, No. 14; part 4, No. 32, parag, 9; *Orah Ḥayyim*, part 1, No. 113 [Hebrew].

3. Henkin, Yehudah, "Is Handshaking a Torah Violation?", *Ḥakira* 4 (Winter 2007), pp. 115-120.

4. Villa, Diana and Susskind Goldberg, Monique, "The Distancing of Menstruants From the Synagogue and Sacred Rites", *To Learn and To Teach*, No. 5, Jerusalem, 2007.

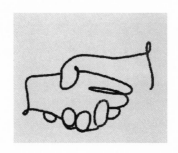

GLOSSARY

Aḥiezer: see Grodzinsky.

Arukh Hashulḥan: see Epstein.

Aszod: see *Yehudah Ya'aleh.*

Azulai, Rabbi Ḥayyim Yosef David (*Ḥida*) (Jerusalem and Italy, 1724-1806): He was considered one of the greatest halakhic authorities in the Oriental and Italian Jewish communities. His prolific works include commentaries on the *Shulḥan Arukh*, such as *Birkei Yosef.*

Beit Yosef: See Karo.

Bertinoro, Rabbi Obadiah of (Italy and Israel, ca. 1450-ca. 1516): author of the classic, comprehensive commentary on the *Mishnah*, based on Rashi and Maimonides.

Betzel Haḥokhmah: Responsa by R. Betzalel Stern (Hungary and Jerusalem, 1911-1989).

Birkei Yosef: see Azulai.

Bemar'eh Habazak: Collection of *responsa* to questions by Diaspora Rabbis published by *Eretz-Ḥemdah*, Institute for Advanced Jewish Studies in Jerusalem.

Ein Yitzḥak: Responsa by Rabbi Isaac Elḥanan Spektor (Kovno, 1817-1896).

Epstein, Rabbi Yeḥiel Michal (Novaradok, 1829-1908): author of *Arukh Hashulḥan*, code of Jewish Law on the four sections of the *Shulḥan Arukh*. His purpose was to rule on Jewish law according to the Talmud, Maimonides, the *Rishonim* and the *Shulḥan Arukh* and its commentators.

Even Ha'ezer: the section of the *Shulḥan Arukh* dealing with marriage and divorce.

Feinstein, Rabbi Moshe (Lithuania and New York, 1895-1986): author of the *responsa* collection *Igrot Moshe*. He was one of the leading halakhic authorities of his time. His rulings are accepted in most Orthodox circles around the world.

Gaon, Rav Amram (died ca. 875): *Gaon* of the *yeshivah* in Sura in Babylon. He wrote many *responsa*. In *response* to a request from Spanish Jewry, R. Amram wrote out the text of the daily prayers (*Seder Rav Amram Gaon*), adding halakhic decisions, comments on customs, and other material.

Gerondi, Zeraḥyah ben Isaac Halevi (Spain and France, ca. 1125-1186): also called *Ba'al Hama'or*. He was a Torah and Talmud commentator and a poet.

Gombiner, Abrahan: see *Magen Avraham*.

Grodzinsky, Rabbi Ḥayyim Ozer (Vilna, 1863-1940): *dayyan* in the famous Vilna rabbinic court, his *responsa* appeared in his book *Aḥiezer*.

Ha'amek Davar: *Responsa* by Rabbi Naphtali Tzvi Yehudah Berlin, the *Netziv* (Russia and Poland, 1816-1893).

HaKohen, Rabbi Israel Meir: see *Mishnah Berurah*.

Ha'elef Lekha Shlomo: Collection of *responsa* by Rabbi Solomon Kluger (Poland, 1785-1869).

Hagahot Maimoniot: glosses on Maimonides' *Mishneh Torah* by Rabbi Meir HaKohen of Rothenburg (b. ca. 1260-died together with his family and students in the Rindfleisch pogrom in 1298).

Hai Gaon (Babylon 939-1038): served as *Gaon* of the Talmudic academy of Pumbedita. He is mainly known for his numerous *responsa*. He also wrote legal treatises, commentaries on the *Mishnah* and liturgical poems.

Hoffmann, Rabbi David Tzvi (Hungary and Germany, 1843-1921): He was Rector of the Neo-Orthodox Hildesheimer Rabbinical Seminary in Berlin. His collection of *responsa, Melamed Le-Ho'il*, deals with a wide range of modern problems.

Ḥoshen Mishpat: the section of the *Shulḥan Arukh* dealing with civil law, torts, damages, etc.

Ibn Ezra, Rabbi Abraham (Spain, Europe and England 1089-ca. 1164): He was a poet, grammarian, Biblical commentator, philosopher, translator, astronomer and physician. He wandered throughout Europe, mainly in Italy, but also in France, England, and other places. His Biblical commentary explains the text according to its plain meaning.

Igrot Moshe: see Feinstein.

Isserlein, Rabbi Israel (Austria, 1390-1460): author of the *responsa* collection *Terumat Hadeshen*. Rabbi Joseph Karo and the Rema often ruled according to his opinion.

Josephus Flavius (Israel and Rome, ca. 38-100 CE): Jewish historian. His works are a source, and sometimes the only surviving source, about crucial events from the times of the revolt against the Romans and the destruction of the Temple.

Karo, Rabbi Joseph (Spain and Israel, 1488-1575): wrote a commentary on the *Tur* called *Beit Yosef* and the *Shulḥan Arukh*, to which the Rema's glosses were added, making it the most influential code until today.

Kesef Mishneh: Rabbi Joseph Karo's commentary on Maimonides*' *Mishneh Torah*.

Klein, Rabbi Isaac (Hungary and U.S.A, 1905-1979): After he moved to the United States, he became a prominent rabbi and halakhic authority within Conservative Judaism. He was president of the Rabbinical Assembly (1958-1960), and a member of its Committee on Jewish Law and Standards (1948-1979). He was the author of several books, notably, *A Guide to Jewish Religious Practice* and *Responsa and Halakhic Studies*.

Kook, Rabbi Abraham Isaac (Latvia and Israel, 1865-1935). The first Ashkenazic Chief Rabbi of modern Israel, Rabbi Kook played a major role in the rebirth of Jewish life in modern Israel. He founded the *Yeshivat Merkaz Ha-Rav*, in Jerusalem. Rabbi Kook authored numerous works on a wide variety of subjects, such as philosophy, mysticism, Talmud, *responsa*, and religious poetry.

Luria, Rabbi Isaac (the *Ari Hakadosh*) (Safed 1534-1572): Foremost Jewish mystic and kabbalist in the community of Safed, he is the founder of Lurianic Kabbalah.

Magen Avraham: one of the principal commentaries on *Oraḥ Ḥayyim*, written by Rabbi Abraham Gombiner (Poland, 1637-1683).

Maharam of Rothenburg, Rabbi Meir ben Baruch of Rothenburg (Germany, 1215-1293): one of the major German decisors; he wrote thousands of *responsa*.

Mahari Bruna, R. Yisrael ben R. Ḥayyim (Bruna, Germany and Prague, ca. 1400-ca. 1480): one of the foremost Torah scholars in Germany, who wrote hundreds of *responsa*.

Maharil, Rabbi Jacob ben Moshe Moellin (Germany ca. 1360-1427): authored many *responsa*. *Minhagei Maharil*, compiled by his student R. Zalman, includes his customs, decisions and interpretations.

Maharit, Rabbi Joseph ben Moses of Trani (Safed and Constantinople, 1568-1639): head of the *yeshivot* in both communities and also leader of the Constantinople community. He wrote numerous *responsa*.

Maimonides (Rambam), Rabbi Moses ben Maimon (Spain and Egypt, 1135-1204): physician, philosopher and halakhic authority; he is the author of the *Mishneh Torah*, which summarizes the entire oral law clearly and concisely in Mishnaic Hebrew. Maimonides also wrote commentaries on the *Mishnah* and the Talmud, *responsa*, philosophical works (such as *The Guide of the Perplexed*) and medical works.

Manoaḥ of Narbonne (Provence end of 13th and first half of 14th century): wrote a commentary on Maimonides' *Mishneh Torah* entitled *Sefer Hamenuḥah*.

Mekhilta deRabbi Yishma'el: a Tannaitic *midrash* on the book of Exodus from the academy of Rabbi Yishma'el.

Melamed Le-Ho'il: See Hoffmann.

Meiri, Rabbi Menahem ben Shlomo Hameiri (Provence, 1249-1315): author of *Beit Habeḥirah*, a commentary on most of the tractates of the Talmud.

Mishnah Berurah: a widely-accepted commentary by Rabbi Israel Meir HaKohen, known as the *Ḥafetz Ḥayyim* (Poland, 1839-1933), on the *Shulḥan Arukh*, *Oraḥ Ḥayyim*.

Mishneh Halakhot: *Responsa* by Rabbi Menashe Klein (Slovakia and New York, b. 1925). After the *Shoah*, he moved to New York where he established the Ungvar community in Boro Park. In addition to *Mishneh Halakhot*, he has written and published works on many aspects of the Torah.

Mishpat Kohen: *Responsa* collection by R. Abraham Isaac Kook. See Kook.

Mishpetei Uzziel: see Uzziel.

Nahmanides (Ramban), Rabbi Moses ben Naḥman (Spain and Israel, 1194-1270): doctor, kabbalist, commentator, poet and authority in Jewish law. He wrote a commentary on the Torah, *novellae* on the Talmud, *responsa* and commentaries on the classical code of the Rif and on Maimonides' *Book of Commandments*.

Noda Bi-Yehudah: *Responsa* collection written by R. Ezekiel ben Judah Landau (Poland, 1713-1793).

Oraḥ Ḥayyim: the section of the *Shulḥan Arukh* dealing with prayer, Shabbat and the Holidays.

Or Zaru'a: a code written by R. Isaac of Vienna (ca. 1180-ca. 1250). It includes legal rulings, commentaries and *responsa* based on the writings of the Ashkenazic *Rishonim*. Many important decisors quoted his rulings.

Pitḥei Teshuvah: Commentary of R. Abraham Zvi Hirsh Eisenstadt (Lithuania, 1813-1868) on the entire *Shulḥan Arukh* except for *Oraḥ Ḥayyim*.

Ra'avan HaYarḥi, **Rabbi Abraham ben R. Nathan** (Provence and Spain, ca. 1155-1215): During his wanderings, he noted the differences in custom between various communities, and later composed *Manhig Bnei Ha'olam* (also known as *Sefer HaManhig*) recording them. In this book, he details various customs and their sources, and sets down his own halachic decisions.

Radbaz, **Rabbi David ibn Zimra** (Spain and Israel, 1479-1573): He is noted for his commentary on Maimonides' *Mishneh Torah* and for his *responsa.*

Rashba, **Rabbi Shlomo ben Aderet** (Spain 1235-1310): Talmudic commentator and author of thousands of *responsa.*

Rashbash, **Rabbi Shlomo ben Shimon Duran** (Algier 1400-1467): known primarily for his *responsa.*

Rashi, **Rabbi Shlomo Yitzḥaki** (France, 1040-1105): his commentaries to the Bible and Talmud are the standard commentaries until today.

Rav Pe'alim: *Responsa* authored by Rabbi Joseph Ḥayyim of Baghdad (ca. 1835-1909).

Rema, Rabbi Moses Isserles (Poland, 1525-1572): author of *Darkhei Moshe* on the *Arba'ah Turim* (see *Tur*) by Jacob ben Asher, and of glosses to the *Shulḥan Arukh* known as the *Mappah* (Tablecloth). These glosses supplemented R. Joseph Karo's code with the laws and customs of Germany, France and Poland. In this way, they contributed to its becoming authoritative throughout the Jewish world in the sixteenth century and until today.

Ribash, **Rabbi Isaac ben Sheshet Perfet** (Spain and Algeria, 1326-1408): He served as a rabbi in Spain and as Chief Rabbi and head of the Rabbinic Court in Algiers. He is the author of the *Responsa* of the *Ribash*, which is an important source of the *Shulḥan Arukh.*

Rishonim, legal authorities who lived ca. 1000-1500.

Ritva, **Rabbi Yom Tov ben Avraham Ishbili** (Spain ca. 1250-ca. 1320): Commentator of the Talmud and author of *halakhic responsa.*

Rosh, **Rabbi Asher ben Yeḥiel** (Germany and Spain, ca. 1250-1327): important decisor who combined the German and Spanish schools of *halakhah*. His major code was *Piskei Ha-Rosh*. He also wrote *novellae* on the Talmud and many *responsa*.

Shakh (Siftei Kohen), **R. Shabbetai ben Meir HaKohen** (Lithuania, 1621-1662): one of the most important commentaries on *Shulḥan Arukh Yoreh De'ah*.

Shevet Halevi: Collection of *responsa* by Rabbi Shmuel HaLevi Wosner (b. Vienna 1914). Rabbi Wosner lives in Bnei Brak (Israel) and is considered one of the preeminent halachic decisors of today.

Shulḥan Arukh: see Karo.

Shulḥan Arukh Harav: Composed by Rabbi Shneur Zalman of Lyady (Russia, 1745-1813). He founded the *Chabad* movement and authored the *Tanya*, the central work of *Chabad Ḥassidism*.

Tam, **Rabbeinu Jacob ben Meir** (France, 1100-1171): Rashi's grandson, one of the most important Tosafists. He was a well-known halakhic authority and many of his *novellae* are included in the commentaries of the Tosafists on the Talmud. He wrote *Sefer Hayashar* which includes *novellae* and *responsa*.

Tashbetz: *Responsa* by Rabbi Shimon ben Tzemach Duran (*Rashbatz*) (Majorca and Algiers, 1361-1444). R. Shimon succeeded Ribash as Chief Rabbi and head of the rabbinical court of Algiers.

Taz (Turei Zahav), **Rabbi David HaLevi** (Poland, 1586-1667): is one of the most immportant commentaries on the *Shulḥan Arukh*.

Terumat Hadeshen: see Isserlein.

Tzitz Eliezer: see Waldenberg.

Tur, **Rabbi Jacob ben Asher** (Germany and Spain, 1269-1343): author of *Arba'ah Turim*, in which he codified the halakhic material up to the fourteenth century and ruled in matters of *halakhah*, placing his father the Rosh in a privileged position.

Unterman, Rabbi Isser Yehudah (Lithuania, England and Israel 1886-1976): He was the Head Rabbi in Liverpool England for 22 years, then became the Chief Rabbi in Tel Aviv and then the Ashkenazic Chief Rabbi of Israel from 1964 until 1972.

Uzziel (Ouziel), Rabbi Ben-Zion Meir Ḥai (Jerusalem, 1880-1953), first Sephardic Chief Rabbi of Israel, author of the *responsa* collection *Mishpetei Uzziel*.

Vilna Gaon, Rabbi Eliyahu of Vilna, the Gra (Vilna, 1720-1797): Rabbi Elijah son of Solomon, one of the most important talmudic scholars and head of the *Mitnagdim* (opponents to the Hassidic movement). He wrote many commentaries, including his commentary *Be'ur Ha'Gra* on the *Shulḥan Arukh*.

Waldenberg, Rabbi Eliezer Yehudah (Jerusalem 1916-2006): *dayyan* and head of a Rabbinical Court in Jerusalem, a judge on the Supreme Rabbinical Court in Jerusalem, and the Rabbi of *Sha'arei Zedek* Medical Center in Jerusalem. He authored a 22-volume collection of *responsa* entitled *Tzitz Eliezer*. His *responsa* deal with all aspects of Jewish Law, but most prominent are his *responsa* dealing with medical problems and new technologies.

Yalkut Yosef: Explanation of the Laws in the *Shulḥan Arukh* based on the halakhic rulings of R. Ovadiah Yosef, written by his son R. Yitzḥak Yosef.

Yaskil Avdi: *Responsa* by Rabbi Ovadiah Hadaya (1890-1969).

Yeḥaveh Da'at: see Yosef.

Yehudah Ya'aleh: *Responsa* by Rabbi Judah Aszod (Hungary, 1794-1866).

Yoreh De'ah: the section of the *Shulḥan Arukh* dealing with *kashrut*, conversion, circumcision, mourning, etc.

Yosef, Rabbi Ovadiah (b. Iraq, 1920): former Sephardic Chief Rabbi of Israel and the *Shas* movement's authority on Jewish Law. Author of *responsa Yabi'a Omer* and *Yeḥaveh Da'at*.

Miriam Berkowitz, *Taking the Plunge: A Practical and Spiritual Guide to the Mikveh*, edited by David Golinkin, Jerusalem, 2007, xvii+187 pp.; second edition, Jerusalem, 2009, xvii+194 pp.

David Golinkin, *The Status of Women in Jewish Law: Responsa*, Jerusalem, 2001, liv+250 pp. (Hebrew with English summaries)

Monique Susskind Goldberg and Diana Villa, *Ask the Rabbi: Women Rabbis Respond to Modern Halakhic Questions*, edited by David Golinkin and Israel Warman, Jerusalem, 2010

Monique Susskind Goldberg and Diana Villa, *Jewish Law Watch: The Agunah Dilemma*, edited by David Golinkin, Nos. 1-7, January 2000 - July 2003 (Hebrew and English)

Monique Susskind Goldberg and Diana Villa, *To Learn and To Teach: Study Booklets Regarding Women in Jewish Law*, edited by David Golinkin, Nos. 1-5, April 2004 - January 2008 (Hebrew, English, French, Spanish, Russian)

Monique Susskind Goldberg and Diana Villa, *Za'akat Dalot: Halakhic Solutions for the Agunot of Our Time*, Jerusalem, 2006, 16+426 pp. (Hebrew with English summaries)

The Schechter Institute of Jewish Studies, Inc., a tax-exempt organization, supports four *amutot* (non-profits) based in Jerusalem, which teach Jewish studies to over 42,000 Jews throughout Israel and Europe. At the Schechter Institute of Jewish Studies, a Graduate School for Israeli educators, over 600 students learn Jewish studies within a pluralistic environment. It includes Applied Research Institutes in *Halakhah*, Women in Jewish Law, and Judaism and the Arts. The Schechter Rabbinical Seminary, affiliated with the Jewish Theological Seminary and the *Masorti*/Conservative movement in Israel, trains rabbis for Israel and the Diaspora. The TALI Education Fund provides enriched Jewish studies for 40,000 Israeli children in 190 state schools and kindergartens. Midreshet Yerushalayim runs outreach activities for Russian immigrants in Israel and veteran Israelis and for Jewish communities in the Ukraine and Hungary. All of these programs advance the struggle for Jewish knowledge and religious pluralism in Israel and throughout the world.

Schechter Institute of Jewish Studies, Inc.

P.O. Box 8500, Philadelphia, PA 19178-3566

Tel.: 866-830-3321, 215-830-1119; Fax: 215-830-0351

Email: schechter@jtsa.edu   www.schechter.edu